THE ELEVENTH AMENDMENT AND SOVEREIGN IMMUNITY

Clyde E. Jacobs

Contributions in American History
Number 19

Greenwood Press, Inc.
Westport, Connecticut

Library of Congress Cataloging in Publication Data

Jacobs, Clyde Edward, 1925-
    The Eleventh amendment and sovereign immunity.

    (Contributions in American history, no. 19)
    Bibliography: p.
    1. Government liability—United States. I. Title.
KF1322.J3   342'.73'088   71-149959
ISBN 0-8371-6058-8

KF1322
J3

Library of Congress Catalog Number: 71-149959
ISBN: 0-8371-6058-8

First published in 1972

Greenwood Press, Inc.
The Publishing Division
51 Riverside Avenue, Westport, Connecticut 06880

Printed in the United States of America

For
Harry C. Jacobs, 1882-1964, and
Jessie Tarbill Jacobs
in appreciation

Contents

Preface

Over a century ago, in his first annual message to Congress, President Lincoln stated: "It is as much the duty of Government to render prompt justice against itself in favor of its citizens as it is to administer the same between private individuals. The investigation and adjudication of claims in their nature belong to the judicial department." Although the duty to which Lincoln referred has been widely acknowledged, it sometimes has not been fulfilled as the national government and the states have successfully pleaded immunity from judicial process. The immunity doctrine, to be sure, has been much constricted during the past hundred years, as courts and legislatures have perceived its mischief in a system professing to be based upon the rule of law. Nevertheless, it is a tenacious doctrine, to which the judiciary occasionally—and unexpectedly—resorts to deny substantial justice to individuals with legal claims upon the government.

Survival of the doctrine, in face of almost universal disapprobation of its rationale and practical effects, is in large measure due to its association with the Constitution. According to traditional theory, the Constitution's delegations of judicial power to the

United States are implicitly circumscribed by the exemption of the sovereign, whether the nation or the states, from unconsented suits by individuals. Adoption of the Eleventh Amendment has been repeatedly cited as declaratory of this implicit limitation, which the Court, at an early time, mistakenly transgressed. To this view, the present study takes exception.

I want to thank the editor of the *American Journal of Legal History* for permission to use in chapter 3 material that first appeared in the *American Journal of Legal History* 12 (January 1968): 19-40.

I am indebted to Professor Louis Loeb, American University, and to Professor Stanley Bernstein, Rutgers University, for having reviewed portions of the manuscript. A grant from the Institute of Social Sciences, University of California, Berkeley, facilitated access to valuable archival materials. Mrs. Roberta Kenney's services as typist are gratefully acknowledged.

CLYDE E. JACOBS
Davis, California
November 1970

THE
ELEVENTH
AMENDMENT
AND
SOVEREIGN IMMUNITY

1

Sovereign Immunity, the States, and the Constitution

Article III of the United States Constitution extends the judicial power of the United States to "Controversies between a State and Citizens of another State . . . and between a State . . . and foreign States, Citizens or Subjects." Despite the superficial clarity and literal breadth of these provisions, contradictory interpretations as to their meaning developed early. The disagreement centered on whether this grant of judicial power subjected the states to suit by citizens of other states and by aliens in federal court. Or, to put the issue another way, was this grant of power implicitly qualified by the doctrine of sovereign immunity?

The first great contest between the Court and the states occurred in 1793 when the Supreme Court of the United States held that a state could be sued by a citizen of another state or by an alien.[1] That contest was speedily resolved, at least nominally, in favor of the states by proposal and ratification of the Eleventh Amendment declaring that "the judicial power of the United States shall not be construed to extend to any suit in law or equity, commenced or prosecuted against one of the United States by Citizens of another State, or by Citizens or Subjects of any Foreign State."

Although a few jurists and historians have contended, principally upon the basis of a literal reading of Article III—and for this reason not persuasively—that the Court decided the issue correctly, this conclusion has not been widely accepted. The ease with which the amendment won approval, probably more than anything else, accounts for the assumption by some commentators that it restored the original intent of the framers of the Constitution by reversing the Court's misinterpretation of Article III. Others, without committing themselves on whether the Court was right or wrong in its reading of the disputed clauses, have argued that the amendment was adopted to enable the states to escape payment of their accumulated debts.

Neither of these views is acceptable. It can be argued that the Court's initial construction of the provisions of Article III was altogether consonant with the intent of the framers and that subsequent adoption of the Eleventh Amendment reversing that interpretation was in response to political and economic considerations differing from those prevailing when the Constitution was drafted and ratified. Moreover, the rather simplistic view that the purpose of the amendment was to relieve the states of an enforceable obligation to pay their debts seems scarcely tenable in the light of various factors, including the strong support it received from creditor-oriented Federalist majorities in Congress and in a number of state legislatures.

Those who framed the Constitution did not write on a blank slate. English political and legal institutions, more than a century and a half of colonial experience, the upheavals of a revolution sealed by a debilitating war, the trauma of independence newly attained, and, indeed, "the felt needs of the time"—all converged to shape the perceptions and the objectives of those who worked through the late spring and summer of 1787 to draft a new instrument of government for the United States.

The English common law was an important part of the heritage of those who drafted the Constitution, so much so that various provisions of the document are virtually unintelligible if read in any other context. Although the common law was introduced slowly in the American colonies and was substantially modified and adapted to local conditions and needs,[2] its general principles were well understood by American lawyers by the second half of the eighteenth century. In their recurrent disputes with the mother country, the colonists asserted the rights of Englishmen, as well as the rights of man, and, in making claim to the former, they studied English law with fervor.[3] As Edmund Burke commented, the love of the colonists for liberty was attributable in no small measure to their study of the law.[4]

The doctrine of sovereign immunity was firmly embedded in the English common law long before the discovery and settlement of the American colonies. So, too, were many of the principles and procedures whereby the doctrine was, in practice, qualified. At least as early as the thirteenth century, during the reign of Henry III (1216-1272), it was recognized that the king could not be sued in his own courts, but this immunity did not imply that the sovereign was above the law. To the contrary, the king was regarded as the fountain of justice and, as such, bound by law and conscience to redress wrongs done to his subjects. This conception appears to account for the initial development of remedies against the ruling sovereign as these began to take shape during the reign of Edward I (1272-1307).[5]

By the time of the American Revolution, a variety of procedures were available for redress of wrongs suffered by the subject at the hands of his sovereign. The petition of right and the *monstrans de droit,*[6] involving proceedings against the crown by name, were already ancient remedies by the eighteenth century. Moreover, the subject could obtain redress by suits for damages against subordinate officers and by means of the various prerogative writs. By the late seventeenth and eighteenth centuries, the Court of Exchequer had entertained actions by the subject for restitution of property wrongfully claimed by the king and for fulfillment of a monetary obligation upon which the crown had defaulted.[7] The immunity doctrine by this time was largely a legal conception, which determined the forms of procedure in some cases but did not seriously impair the subject's right to recovery in accordance with the substantive law.

Even the petition of right—the mode of redress most closely associated with the doctrine of sovereign immunity—was, from an early time, a regularized legal procedure for securing relief from the king. While the king was legally entitled to deny the petition, thereby preventing redress of the wrong, it appears that the sovereign's assent to proceedings against himself in his own courts was, in practice, granted or withheld not as a matter of unfettered royal discretion but upon the basis of law—that is, upon the basis of whether the petition made out a *prima facie* legal claim for redress.[8] Once a petition of right received royal endorsement, a commission issued for an inquest to ascertain the facts. When the facts were found, and perhaps after some additional prodding, the crown answered the petitioner's plea and the case was tried before the King's Bench or some other tribunal. Although the king enjoyed many procedural advantages in the trial, the courts dispensed relief generally in accordance with the substantive law. Redress by petition of right was a slow, cumbersome, and costly proceeding, and largely because of this, the petition was, for a time, eclipsed as a remedy by more expeditious procedures. But underlying the petition of right was a vital principle: a subject with a legal claim against the king was as much entitled to redress as if the claim were against a fellow subject.[9] This principle survived the temporary decline of the petition and accounted for the development of other modes of redress in the seventeenth and eighteenth centuries, as well as for the revival of the petition, in its modern form, in the nineteenth century.[10]

Probably no one would maintain that the highly developed, sophisticated modes of redress available to the subject against the king and his subordinates were transplanted intact in the American colonies. Conclusions concerning the extent to which these technical procedures were understood and invoked by the colonists must await a comprehensive study of colonial records. It is clear, however, that American lawyers of the Revolutionary period were familiar not only with the abstract doctrine of sovereign immunity but with principles that circumscribed that doctrine. The American edition of Sir William Blackstone's *Commentaries on the Laws of England* was published in 1771 and 1772; this treatise, whatever its scholarly limitations, exercised great influence in the colonies. Burke estimated that nearly as many copies of Blackstone were sold in the colonies as in the mother country, and he noted the tendencies of colonial laymen to become "smatterers in law."[11]

In a famous passage in the *Commentaries*, Blackstone stated the immunity doctrine and its limitations.[12] From the maxim that the king can do no wrong, he argued simply that "whatever may be amiss in the conduct of public affairs is not chargeable personally on the king, nor is he, or his ministers, accountable for it to the people." However, the royal prerogative does not extend to do any injury because it was created to benefit the people. Hence, where by "misinformation or inadvertence" the crown violates private rights, though no compulsory process lies against the king, the law affords redress by way of petition of right. For the sovereign to know of the injury and to redress it are inseparable, and once the injury is made known, the petition is granted by the king as a matter of course and his judges directed to do justice to the aggrieved party. For Blackstone, as for earlier jurists and commentators, the doctrine of sovereign immunity was simply a way of stating that the king was not amenable to the jurisdiction of his own courts unless he assented to such jurisdiction. However, the doctrine was not then understood as relieving the sovereign of his legal obligations or even as defining the scope of his liability— if, indeed, it was ever so understood.[13] Once jurisdiction was asserted, the courts measured the conflicting claims of subject and sovereign according to the principles of law and equity. And, even though the king might legally refuse to be impleaded, Blackstone and others assumed that the sovereign would do justice whenever a valid claim arose. The very existence of a subject's legal right supposed legal redress for the wrong he had suffered. This was nothing less than a premise of English law, stated earlier in the century by Chief Justice John Holt: "If the plaintiff has a right, he must of necessity have means of vindication if he is injured in the exercise or enjoyment of it. Right and remedy, want of right and want of remedy, are reciprocal."[14]

With the attainment of independence, some of the former colonists soon discovered that right and remedy were not reciprocal, at least insofar as the obligations of government toward the individual were concerned. Largely as a consequence of the war, the states, as well as the Continental Congress, had accumulated substantial debts owed to both foreign and domestic creditors. Although the financial policies of the states and of the central government during the Confederation period were not as irresponsible as sometimes portrayed,[15] public and private creditors were at least concerned and often alarmed by those policies. With no power to levy taxes, the Confederation government was in dire financial straits; and, after a time, it defaulted upon much of its accumulated debt.[16] The states were potentially in a better financial position, and a few, in fact, made substantial progress in retiring their debts upon a basis satisfactory to their creditors. Others, however, defaulted or resorted to putting into circulation new paper money as a painless way of meeting their obligations.[17] Dissatisfied creditors could petition for satisfaction, but they lacked an enforceable, legal remedy.

Moreover, some perceived that failure to pay the public debt created problems transcending the private interests of creditors clamoring for relief. Default upon that portion of the debt owed to foreign governments and subjects posed international dangers.

And, because domestic creditors were concentrated in a few states, the failure of debtor states other than their own to fulfill financial obligations was recognized as a potential source of interstate friction. Satisfaction of the debts owed by the Confederation and by the states was viewed as a precondition for peace and harmony, both at home and abroad.

The movement for reform of the Articles of Confederation, and, as it turned out, for a new instrument of government was partly due to solicitude for the creditor and to fears of the larger dangers that might ensue from default upon the public debt. The legacy of these concerns is readily discerned in constitutional provisions enlarging the legislative powers of the central government, laying certain prohibitions upon the states, and recognizing the Confederation debt. Those clauses of Article III extending the judicial power of the United States to controversies between a state and citizens of other states or aliens may be read in the same light, and a review of the movement for reform of the Articles and of the proceedings at Philadelphia supports this interpretation.

The judicial power of the United States under the Articles of Confederation was far from being coextensive with the legislative power vested in the Congress, and the courts of the Confederation had only a most restricted jurisdiction. Congress could appoint courts for the trial of piracies and felonies on the high seas and for appeals in all cases of captures. In addition, it could establish ad hoc tribunals with jurisdiction over controversies between two or more states and over disputes between individuals claiming land under the different grants of two or more states—although the process was cumbersome.[18] The Confederation government was otherwise dependent upon the state judiciaries for settling controversies having interstate or international ramifications, as well as for disposing of cases arising under the Articles and the ordinances and treaties of the United States.

Although failure to provide for the establishment of a Confederation judiciary with extensive jurisdiction was, from the first, a source of embarrassment to the central government, early criticism of the Articles centered largely on the weakness of Congress and the inadequacy of the nascent executive authority of the government. In 1780, even before final ratification of the Articles, Alexander Hamilton urged sweeping revisions and criticized the "want of power in Congress" and the "want of method and energy in the administration";[19] but he made no mention of the weaknesses of the judiciary provision.

Later, however, Hamilton recognized, as did other nationalists, that an organized judiciary with broad powers was an essential part of a self-sufficing central government. As a delegate from New York to the Confederation Congress in 1783, Hamilton presented a series of resolutions calling upon the states to appoint a convention to propose and adopt such alterations in the Articles as might be necessary. Among the twelve defects Hamilton cited was the following:

> Thirdly: In want of a Federal Judicature, having cognizance of all matters of general concern in the last resort, especially those in which foreign nations and their subjects are interested; from which defect, by the interference of the local regulations of particular States militating directly or indirectly against the powers vested in the Union, the national treaties will be liable to be infringed, the national faith to be violated, and public tranquillity to be disturbed.[20]

This resolution was addressed to both a particular and a general problem. Hamilton was concerned specifically with the relationship between Confederation treaties and conflicting state legislation—a matter which was soon to engage his attention as an attorney and advocate.[21] Moreover, in a broader sense, the resolution reflects the nationalist view that a federal judiciary endowed with broad jurisdiction was indispensable to maintaining international peace and domestic tranquillity. In either sense, Hamilton's ideas anticipated those of most other nationalist delegates at the Philadelphia Convention four years later.

Although Hamilton's proposals were not favorably received by Congress, the inadequacy of the federal judiciary was too evident to escape official attention. In August 1786, a grand committee of the Confederation Congress reported a series of proposed amendments to the Articles.[22] Among these was a resolution to empower Congress to establish a court of seven judges, appointed on a geographic basis. This court was to be invested with original jurisdiction over criminal prosecutions against federal officers and with appellate powers in "all causes wherein questions shall arise on the meaning and construction of treaties entered into by the United States with any foreign power, or on the law of nations, or wherein any question shall arise respecting any regulations that may hereafter be made by Congress relative to trade and commerce, or the collection of federal revenues pursuant to powers that shall be vested in that body or wherein questions of importance may arise and the United States shall be a party."[23] Nothing came of the committee's proposals, however, because, by the date scheduled for their discussion, Congress was deeply immersed in debate over negotiations with Spain concerning commerce and navigation of the Mississippi, and the initiative for change was soon to pass to the Annapolis, and subsequently, the Philadelphia Convention.

The direction of nationalist thought regarding the judiciary was indicated, almost on the eve of the Philadelphia Convention, by James Madison in a letter to George Washington.[24] National supremacy, Madison wrote, should extend to the judicial branch, for if those who expound and apply the laws are connected by their oaths and interests wholly with the particular states and not with the Union, the national legislative power might be rendered "unavailing." To prevent this, Madison suggested that "the oaths of the judges should include a fidelity to the general as well as local constitution, and that an appeal should lie to some national tribunals in all cases to which foreigners or inhabitants of other states" may be parties and to cases in admiralty jurisdiction. The requisite judicial power of the Union and the jurisdiction of the federal courts would accordingly embrace two classes of cases. The first area of national concern was those cases in which the supremacy of national law—presumably constitutional, statutory, and treaty law—would be endangered by the parochialism of state judges. Here the minimum solution was to require these judges to subscribe to oaths in support of the Union. As a second area of national concern, Madison points to *all* cases involving foreigners and citizens of other states—cases where the supremacy of national law might not be directly threatened but where decisions by state judges could disrupt international peace and domestic harmony. In such cases, national tribunals should have appellate jurisdiction.

Whether Madison thought that federal courts should possess any jurisdiction over suits instituted against a state by citizens of another state or by foreigners must remain a matter of some conjecture; indeed there is no direct evidence that he considered the question at all. The doctrine of sovereign immunity, and the principles limiting that immunity were, as we have noticed, well established at the time Madison wrote, and, during the Confederation period, the doctrine had been successfully invoked by at least one state.[25] It is possible that Madison regarded the doctrine as controlling—thereby creating an implied exception to the sweeping jurisdiction that he appears to have proposed. If such was his view, then the federal appellate power presumably would extend only to those cases in which a state initiated a suit against a noncitizen or a foreigner, and, possibly, to cases where citizens of different states were adverse parties. Later, during debate over ratification of the Constitution in the Virginia convention, Madison argued that the states were immune, but these remarks may have been merely a belated concession to the opposition.

There is still another hypothesis regarding Madison's meaning, even though it seems extremely tenuous. Madison may have seen in the proposed federal appellate power a means whereby the sovereign immunity of the states in their dealings with noncitizens and foreigners could be given national sanction, thereby reducing the possibility of interstate and international friction. Scarcely six years before the letter to Washington was written, a case that posed a serious threat to relations between his own state, Virginia, and the Commonwealth of Pennsylvania was decided in a Philadelphia court. In this case, *Nathan* v. *Virginia,*[26] a foreign attachment had been issued against the Commonwealth of Virginia at the suit of Simon Nathan, and a quantity of imported clothing belonging to the state was attached by the sheriff in Philadelphia. The case aroused concern on the part of Virginia's delegates to the Confederation Congress, and they applied to the Supreme Executive Council of Pennsylvania for suppression of the attachment on the ground that the law of nations was violated by seizure of the property of a sovereign state. The council then directed the sheriff who had executed the process to suppress the attachment and to surrender the goods, and Nathan sought relief in the Court of Common Pleas. After hearing elaborate argument, the court sustained the state's claim to immunity, and the matter was settled. Had the decision gone the other way in the Pennsylvania courts, a serious breach of relations between the two states might have occurred, and it is by no means certain that the Confederation government would have had any appellate power over a dispute of this kind.[27]

Close analysis of Madison's letter suggests, however, that he was in fact contemplating a very broad grant of jurisdiction to federal tribunals, and the whole thrust of nationalist thinking at the time went counter to the notion of state sovereignty. It was Madison who was soon to press strongly for a national negative on state legislation and for an extraordinarily sweeping grant of legislative authority to the central government.[28] In light of these proposals, the latitude of his language concerning the proposed federal judiciary should not be discounted, whatever his disclaimers may have been at a later time, for Madison and other nationalists believed that the federal judiciary should be armed with powers not only to maintain the supremacy of national law but also to review state judicial decisions that might have interstate or foreign ramifications. Thus one of the principal reasons nationalists advanced for extending the federal judicial power—the maintenance of international peace and domestic harmony—would appear to necessitate national jurisdiction in cases where the good faith of the states vis-à-vis foreigners and citizens of other states had been engaged. If, however, this proposed federal judicial jurisdiction were qualified by the doctrine of state immunity, a broad avenue would have been left open to defeat every claim made upon them by citizens of other states and by aliens. The exception to the jurisdiction would have made the proposed jurisdiction futile or, at least, negligible.

Regardless of whether the financial policies of the states were actually as chaotic as critics of the Confederation claimed, the important fact is that Madison and other nationalists were convinced that those policies would create serious discord at home and abroad. During the same month that he wrote to Washington, Madison penned a short note expressing some of his concerns and suggesting additional safeguards.[29] "Paper money, installments of debts, occlusion of courts, making property a legal tender" are aggressions upon the rights of other states and upon foreign nations, for the citizens of every state, in the aggregate, stand in the relation of creditors or debtors to the citizens of every other state. When a debtor state acts in favor of debtors, such acts "affect the creditor state in the same manner as they do its own citizens." Madison feared the frauds upon the citizens of other states and upon foreign subjects because legislation in favor of debtors might disturb the domestic tranquillity and involve the Union in foreign contests. Madison's note no doubt relates primarily to the policies of some of the states regarding the settlement of private debts, and the Philadelphia Convention, in drafting the Constitution, was soon to erect important safeguards against state interference in behalf of private debtors.[30] But the principal purpose of such safeguards, as understood by Madison and other nationalists—to prevent frauds by the states upon non-citizens and foreigners in order to alleviate interstate and foreign friction—also supports a grant of power to the federal government with respect to the settlement of the states' public obligations toward foreigners and citizens of other states. The Judiciary Article of the Constitution, with reference to certain assignments of judicial power to the United States, may be construed in light of this seemingly transcendent objective.

The Philadelphia Convention assembled on May 14, 1787, but it did not begin its deliberations until May 25 when, for the first time, delegates from nine states were present. Four days later, Edmund Randolph of Virginia "opened the main business" by presenting a brief criticism of the Confederation government, together with a series of fifteen resolutions proposing changes designed to remedy the defects of the existing government. Among these resolutions (probably written by Madison) was one calling for the institution of one or more supreme courts, as well as inferior tribunals, the former to have appellate, and the latter, original jurisdiction "to hear and determine all piracies and felonies on the high seas; captures from an enemy; *cases in which foreigners, or citizens of other States, applying to such jurisdictions, may be interested;* or which respect the collection of national revenue; impeachments of any national officers, and questions which may involve the national peace and harmony."[31]

From the outset, then, the nationalists wanted extensive jurisdiction in the federal courts; and the broad language of Randolph's resolution anticipated in a general way the specific assignments of judicial power to the central government detailed in Article III of the Constitution. Many years later Madison was to write that the Randolph resolutions were a "mere sketch in which omitted details were to be supplied."[32] The resolution on the judiciary, however, indicates that the nationalists desired a federal judicial power that could reach those matters transcending, in any manner, the interests of individual states vis-à-vis their own citizens. And it is at least worth notice that the proposal to invest federal courts with jurisdiction over cases involving foreigners and citizens of other states may readily be interpreted as including cases in which such persons instituted proceedings against a state, although this is not made explicit.

The first discussion of Randolph's judiciary resolution, on June 4 and 5, centered largely on the manner of selecting federal judges; only scant attention was given to the scope of the judicial power. Debate on the judiciary thereafter seems to have been episodic and somewhat desultory. On June 12, Randolph's proposal on judicial power was at least tentatively modified when the convention, in committee of the whole, voted to delete the references to "piracies and felonies on the high seas" and "all captures from an enemy."[33] Moreover, they approved a change substituting for "other states" the phrase "two distinct states of the Union."[34] This amendment was significant: the now-modified Randolph resolution extended the federal judicial power to cases between individuals from different states, but the change appears to have simultaneously withdrawn inferential jurisdiction over cases in which a state and a citizen of another state were the adverse parties.[35] The following day the delegates, again sitting as the committee of the whole, overrode the decision, voting without dissent to strike out the entire clause relating to the jurisdiction of the federal courts in order to leave "full room for their organization." The committee then voted, upon motion by Randolph and Madison, a much simpler resolution providing "that the jurisdiction of the national judiciary shall extend to cases which respect the collection of the national revenue, impeachments of any national officers, and questions which involve the national peace and harmony."[36] In this form, the committee of the whole again reported the resolution to the convention.

Before any further discussion of the Randolph plan took place, William Paterson of New Jersey and Alexander Hamilton presented alternative proposals, both providing for a national judiciary with enlarged powers. Neither of these plans, however, would have assigned to the federal courts a jurisdiction as broad as that indicated by the Randolph resolution. The Paterson plan proposed a single supreme court with original jurisdiction over impeachments of federal officers and final appellate powers "in all cases touching the rights of ambassadors; in all cases of captures from an enemy; in all cases of piracies and felonies on the high seas; in all cases in which foreigners may be interested; in the construction of any treaty or treaties, or which may arise on any of the acts for the regulation of trade, or the collection of the federal revenue."[37] Hamilton also proposed a single court with original jurisdiction in cases of capture and appellate jurisdiction in causes concerning both national revenues and citizens of foreign nations.[38]

Although Hamilton's proposal seems to have evoked little discussion, the Paterson resolution calling for the creation of a single supreme court was the subject of intense debate. On July 18, the convention agreed to a resolution empowering the national legislature to create inferior courts, and the delegates turned again to the problem of jurisdiction. Once again the language of the Randolph resolution was modified and made more general; "that the jurisdiction shall extend to all cases arising under the national laws; and to such other questions as may involve the national peace and harmony."[39]   This resolution, together with those of Paterson and Pinckney, was referred to the Committee of Detail, whose members were John Rutledge, Edmund Randolph, Oliver Ellsworth, Nathaniel Gorham, and James Wilson. The convention adjourned to August 6 to allow the committee time to frame a report.[40]

While the deliberations of the Committee of Detail were not officially recorded, some of its working papers are extant,[41] and these throw some light on the genesis and development of the judiciary provision that was subsequently reported. Both the Paterson and the Pinckney resolutions on the judiciary influenced the final product, but the Randolph resolution seems to have been most important. Randolph's resolution was, as has already been noted, generalized by the convention, but Randolph, as a member of the committee, prepared a rough draft making specific assignments of jurisdiction to the federal judiciary. According to this draft proposal, the jurisdiction of the supreme court was to extend to cases arising under laws passed by the general legislature and to impeachments of officers. Moreover, the national legislature was empowered to vest that tribunal with jurisdiction over such other cases "as involving the national peace and harmony": (1) in collection of revenue, (2) in disputes between citizens of different states, (3) in disputes between different states, and (4) in disputes in which subjects or citizens of other countries are concerned.[42] And to these was added, by way of a marginal note in the handwriting of John Rutledge, the rapporteur of the committee, the clause "in disputes between a state and a citizen or citizens of other states."[43] In what appears to be a later, better polished draft of the committee's report—in the handwriting of James Wilson—this clause, as well as the others, is retained although the jurisdiction is automatically granted subject to legislative exceptions in favor of inferior federal courts.[44]

On the appointed day, August 6, John Rutledge presented to the convention the committee report—a draft constitution of twenty-three articles. Article XI provided for the federal judiciary with the jurisdiction of the Supreme Court defined as follows in the Section 3 of that article:

> The jurisdiction of the Supreme Court shall extend to all cases arising under laws passed by the Legislature of the United States; to all cases affecting ambassadors, other public ministers and consuls; to the trial of impeachments of officers of the United States; to all cases of admiralty and maritime jurisdiction; to controversies between two or more States, (except such as shall regard territory or jurisdiction); *between a state and citizens of another State;* between citizens of different States; and *between a state,* or the citizens thereof, *and foreign states, citizens or subjects.* In cases of impeachment, cases affecting ambassadors, other public ministers and con-

suls, and those in which a State shall be party, this jurisdiction shall be original. In all the other cases before-mentioned, it shall be appellate, with such exceptions, and under such regulations, as the Legislature shall make. The Legislature may assign any part of the jurisdiction above-mentioned (except the trial of the President of the United States) in the manner, and under the limitations which it shall think proper, to such inferior courts, as it shall constitute from time to time.[45]

Here, for the first time, the convention was presented with a proposal explicitly extending the judicial power of the United States to controversies between a state and citizens of other states, as well as foreigners. But this clause, which was incorporated into the final version of the Constitution, seems to have occasioned neither debate nor comment among the delegates, although they participated in wide-ranging discussion of the judiciary article and voted some significant changes. The final approved section of the Constitution concerning the judicial power follows:

The judicial power shall extend to all Cases, in Law and Equity, arising under this Constitution, the Laws of the United States, and Treaties made, or which shall be made, under their Authority; to all Cases affecting Ambassadors, other public Ministers and Consuls;—to all Cases of admiralty and maritime Jurisdiction;—to Controversies to which the United States shall be a Party;—to Controversies between two or more States;—between a State and Citizens of another State;—between Citizens of different States,—between Citizens of the same State claiming Lands under grants of different States, and between a State, or the Citizens thereof, and foreign States, Citizens or Subjects.[46]

An ambiguity remains, however: neither the committee proposal nor the final version of the judiciary article explicitly extends the federal judicial power to cases in which a state is impleaded as a defendant. In the judiciary article there is no differentiation between the states as plaintiffs and the states as defendants. It is possible, however, that the framers of the provision, as well as the delegates who approved it, may have read the clause as extending the judicial power only to cases in which a state was the plaintiff. In other words, they may have presumed that the broad language of the clauses extending the federal judicial power "to controversies between a state and citizens of another state . . . and between a state and foreign states, citizens or subjects" was subject to the implied immunity of a state from suit by any individual. If these clauses are construed in this way, then the federal judicial power would reach only those cases in which a state was plaintiff or in which a state consented to be sued.

To put the argument for reservation of immunity as forcefully as possible, the various assignments of judicial power in Article III—so the argument goes—are subject to the implied qualification that the cases and controversies to which that power is extended are those which can otherwise be maintained under the law. This general proposition is sound enough, but its application may be doubted, since the argument for implied immunity then proceeds on the assumption that a suit against a sovereign state is not maintainable at law, and then to the conclusion that suits against a state are beyond the federal judicial power. But this line of argument, in fact, begs the basic question. The doctrine of sovereign immunity, as noted earlier, does not determine the legal liability of the sovereign, imposed by general principles of substantive law, and the immunity merely precludes resort by the individual to the courts for legal redress. A suit against the sovereign is maintainable if immunity is waived, and such waiver may very well be implicit in an instrument extending the judicial power to controversies between the sovereign and certain individuals. Such, at least, had been the practice in England. In the Tudor period, the Courts of Augmentations, Wards, and Surveyors, created by statute, had entertained legal claims against the crown, and during the seventeenth and eighteenth centuries, the Court of Exchequer had still broader jurisdiction over claims involving the financial obligations of the sovereign to the subject. Still other actions against the sovereign could be instituted in chancery. In light of these precedents, waiver of immunity—rather than a reservation of it—appears to be the better inference from general language extending the judicial power to certain categories of cases.

The question of whether immunity was waived cannot, however, be resolved in favor of implied waiver on this basis alone. Nor can it be settled by a literal reading of the broad language of Article III, although some judges and commentators apparently thought so.[47] If the language extending the federal judicial power to controversies between a state and citizens of other states, by its own force alone, constituted a waiver of the state's immunity from suit, it is not at all clear why the equally explicit clauses of the same section, extending the judicial power to "controversies to which the United States shall be a party" and to "all cases affecting ambassadors, other public ministers, and consuls" did not by the same token waive the immunity of these parties. Probably no one would have seriously contended that diplomatic immunity was or could be waived by Article III. And the idea that the United States was made suable in federal court by reason of that article, while certainly defensible, was eventually rejected.[48] However, concession of immunity to the United States and to foreign diplomatic representatives, under Article III, does not necessitate the conclusion that the states were to be immune under parallel clauses of that article. In at least one class of controversies falling within the federal judicial power—those between two or more states—a waiver of immunity must be conceded. Otherwise the clause extending the judicial power to such cases would be almost meaningless, and the power granted by the Constitution made even less efficacious in this respect than that granted by the Articles of Confederation.

Textual analysis of various provisions of Article III, then, suggests contradictory answers as to whether the states were to retain immunity from suit by individuals; that is, the language of that provision, by itself, yields no answer. Moreover, the records of the convention simply do not cast any direct light on the question, nor does there seem to have been any comment upon the matter in the correspondence of convention delegates. To be sure, a few delegates a short time later, during the debates over ratification, disavowed any intention of investing the federal courts with jurisdiction over suits instituted by an individual against a state. But such disclaimers, occurring under virtual political duress and sharply contested by others, should not be uncritically accepted as accurate representations of the purpose of the provision, either as originally conceived or as understood by those who ratified the Constitution.

Although the records of the convention are barren of any direct reference to the suability of the states under Article III, they nevertheless provide some collateral evidence that the states were to lose their existing immunity.

First, it is clear that the framers of the Constitution attached utmost importance to the fidelity of financial obligations, both public and private. This consideration pervaded their deliberations, and it is unquestionably manifested in various sections of the finished product. The clauses of Article III, if read as depriving the states of their immunity to suit, would be consonant with this fundamental objective. Thus certain creditors—and precisely those who by reason of their noncitizenship would exercise the weakest claims upon the good faith of a debtor state—would be afforded effective redress in an impartial forum.

Second, the genesis of the constitutional provisions concerning the judicial power of the United States casts additional light upon the problem. Even before the convention assembled, criticisms of the Confederation had pointed to the need for a national judiciary having cognizance of matters of national importance. In the first reference to the judiciary in the convention, Randolph urged the creation of federal courts having powers over *cases in which foreigners or citizens of other states, applying to such jurisdictions may be interested, and questions involving the national peace and harmony.* In subsequent debates, there were recurrent references to a judicial power encompassing cases affecting the national peace and harmony, and, as already noted, the delegates approved a generalized resolution to this effect and referred it to the Committee of Detail, where it served as a guideline. It was this committee that drafted the detailed assignments of judicial power, presumably to implement this general objective.

If this objective was controlling in the formulation of the various specific assignments of the federal judicial power, some differentiation between the separate clauses as to the scope and content of each—a differentiation not warranted by the text alone—becomes possible. The clause extending the judicial power to cases affecting diplomatic representatives may be understood as giving the national courts cognizance of such cases, in order to assure, among other things, that the diplomatic immunity existing under international law would be accorded national judicial sanction. This would preclude state judicial action which could endanger international relations and the peace of the Union.

Greater difficulty is encountered in determining whether the United States was to enjoy immunity from suit under the clause granting judicial power "in controversies to which the United States shall be a party." Later judicial statements generally recognized such immunity, commonly on the ground that a government should not be subject to compulsory process in its own courts. This argument is not altogether persuasive, and the conclusion may be incorrect. Still, in the eyes of the framers, allowance of an exemption in favor of the United States might have posed few dangers to national peace and harmony. At best, however, the judicial inference that the United States is immune from suit in its own courts, rests upon nebulous evidence.

A waiver of immunity, on the other hand, must surely be read into the clause extending the federal judicial power to controversies between two or more states. If such waiver is not assumed, then this grant of judicial power would fall far short of attaining its objective of maintaining national peace and harmony, for the ultimate recourse, in the absence of compulsory judicial settlement, in territorial and other disputes between the states would be armed force.

The question remains whether the purpose of the clauses extending the federal judicial power to controversies between a state and citizens of another state or aliens was to provide merely an impartial tribunal for the disposition of suits in which a state was plaintiff or voluntarily appeared, or a tribunal which was open to certain individuals for redress of wrongs committed by the states. The national peace and harmony concededly might be promoted, to a limited extent, by a restrictive interpretation—one supposing the continued immunity of the states from suit by individuals. If interpreted in this way, these clauses would afford an impartial forum for the disposition of suits instituted by a state against the specified parties. Thus, a state would not be required to resort to the courts of a sister state in order to press its claims against noncitizens whose persons and property were located outside its own territorial jurisdiction. Moreover, a noncitizen defendant who resided in the plaintiff state would be afforded an impartial federal tribunal for hearing and judgment on the claim against him.

This restrictive interpretation, however, falls short of fulfilling the broad objectives behind the various specific assignments of the judicial power. Default and repudiation of state debts were in the air, posing serious threats of friction between the states, as well as foreign reprisals. The holders of state obligations were concentrated in a few states, and among the states there were marked differences in attitude toward fulfilling outstanding obligations. Under these circumstances subjection of the states to federal judicial authority probably was deemed essential for preservation of national peace and harmony.

Perhaps the foregoing analysis attributes too much, by way of prescience, to those who authored the Constitution. That they did not, and could not, foresee all the logical and historical consequences of their language is certain. Nor did they anticipate every specific problem over which later constitutional controversies would rage. There is some evidence, however, that those who drafted the clauses extending the federal judicial power to controversies between a state and noncitizens had a definite goal. The subsequent conduct of at least two—and possibly three—of the five members of the Committee of Detail strongly suggests that they did not see the principle of sovereign immunity as a limitation on this grant of power. Edmund Randolph, for example, had presented to the convention the first draft proposal on the powers of the national judiciary, which as generalized by the delegates, stated the objectives for which specific assignments were to be worked out in the committee. Later, Randolph, as a delegate to the Virginia ratification convention, argued repeatedly against the immunity of the states from suit by individuals.[49] And it was Randolph who appeared as counsel for the plaintiff in *Vanstophorst* v. *Maryland,*[50] the first of the suits instituted against a state, and subsequently in *Chisholm* v. *Georgia.*[51] James Wilson, probably the leading legal theorist at the Philadelphia Convention, took a similar position before the ratifying convention in Pennsylvania,[52] and, in 1789 and 1790, while a member of the Pennsylvania state constitutional convention, persuaded that body to write into its document a waiver of the state's immunity from suit in its own courts.[53] Moreover, it was Wilson, who as a member of the Supreme Court of the United States authored, in *Chisholm* v. *Georgia,* the most far-reaching of the opinions sustaining the suability of a state. The views of a third member of the committee, Oliver Ellsworth, were probably much like Randolph's and Wilson's on the question, but evidence of this is less direct and more equivocal.[54]

Finally, it may be argued that a waiver of the states' immunity to suit was consonant with, even if not inherent in, the nature of the constitutional system devised at Philadelphia. The powers delegated to the three branches of the central government constituted, in part, subtractions from the powers of sovereignty of the state *governments,* if not from the sovereignty of the states as such. Even if the ultimate locus of political sovereignty resided in the states or their respective peoples—as it may have under the

Articles of Confederation and, according to compact theory, under the Constitution—the legal sovereignty of the state governments, which was limited under the Articles, was restricted further by the Constitution. Article III of the Constitution extended the judicial power of the United States not only to matters falling within the cognizance of the executive and legislative branches of the central government but also to other matters, where, because of the nature or situation of the parties, it was possible that the national interest might be affected. To the extent that action or inaction by the state governments might undermine that interest, their powers were accordingly restricted.

2

The Judiciary Article and the State Conventions

With the submission of the proposed Constitution for ratification, the period of constitutional formulation ended and a period of justification began. The injunction of secrecy enveloping the proceedings at Philadelphia was partly lifted, and the finished work was bared to public scrutiny. And the nationalists, who preempted the designation "Federalist," were placed on the defensive in some critical areas.

At first, before the forces opposed to the new Constitution were able to group themselves, the Federalists made impressive, virtually unimpeded progress. Within four months after submission, five states had ratified—among them Delaware, New Jersey, and Georgia, where state conventions acted perfunctorily and unanimously. In the other two, Pennsylvania and Connecticut, action was similarly swift, although there was some dissent within the state conventions.

The judiciary article of the proposed Constitution was not the principal object of anti-Federalist attack. Indeed, the anti-Federalists, with some important exceptions, oscillated, on the one hand, between broadside attacks against the "consolidating" tendencies of the document and the allegedly unlawful conduct of its framers, and, on the other hand, criticisms of minutiae.[1] Their most important criticism was the absence of a bill of rights, but they were also concerned about the organization and powers of the political branches of the projected government. When they singled out for attention the judiciary article, they most often objected to the clauses extending the judicial power of the United States to cases arising under its Constitution, laws, and treaties and to controversies involving diversity of citizenship. They regarded the latter, in particular, as a potential source of inconvenience and mischief. Moreover, many considered the absence of a guarantee of trial by jury in civil cases as a serious defect.

The provision vesting in the United States judicial power over controversies between a state and citizens of other states or foreigners aroused diverse comment in some state ratifying conventions, as well as in newspapers and pamphlets published at the time. In at least six states—Pennsylvania, Massachusetts, Virginia, New York, North Carolina, and Rhode Island—the provision received attention. Some ratification advocates construed it as making the states amenable to suit by individuals, but most Federalists, commenting upon the matter, denied this meaning. On the other hand, ratification opponents generally interpreted the provision as constituting a dangerous extension of federal judicial authority. Moreover, a few state conventions, in ratifying the Constitution, voted to recommend amendments that either explicitly or implicitly were designed to divest the federal government of judicial power over controversies of this kind.

Pennsylvania was the first of the large states to ratify the Constitution, and it was the first to record its criticism of the judiciary article. Here, as elsewhere, much of the criticism was ill-defined; generally, the delegates feared that the federal judiciary would absorb the courts of the several states.[2] Specifically, they objected to diversity of citizenship jurisdiction, to the absence of a guarantee to trial by jury in civil cases, and to appeals with respect to fact as well as law.

So far as the fragmentary records of the Pennsylvania convention reveal, there was no serious criticism of the clauses extending the federal judicial power to controversies between a state and citizens of other states or foreigners. However, James Wilson addressed the convention in defense of the provision, and at least one direct reference to the matter appears in one of the pamphlets published in the state.[3]

In a speech closely analyzing specific clauses of the Constitution—and one deemed to have been extraordinarily influential in winning support for ratification—Wilson defended the extension of judicial power to controversies between a state and citizens of another state.[4] "Impartiality," he said, "is the leading feature" of the Constitution, and, when a citizen has a controversy with another state, "there ought to be a tribunal where both parties may stand on a just and equal footing." In defense of the provision conferring diversity jurisdiction in controversies between citizens of different states and between a state or its citizens and foreign states or their subjects, Wilson adverted to the need to restore public and private credit. Foreigners, like American citizens, should have access to a just and impartial tribunal and not have their rights as creditors placed at the mercy of state laws and state tribunals.

Whatever doubts delegates to the Pennsylvania convention may have had regarding the wisdom of extending the judicial power of the United States to controversies between a state and noncitizens seem to have been allayed by the time of adjournment. The anti-Federalist minority proposed fifteen amendments to the Constitution, one of which dealt with the powers of the federal judiciary.[5] This amendment, which was decisively defeated along with the others, would have abolished jurisdiction in controversies between citizens of different states, but no change was even proposed regarding the clause relating to controversies between a state and citizens of other states.[6]

In Massachusetts, Federalist and anti-Federalist forces were closely balanced in the state convention; indeed, at the outset, the latter appeared to enjoy a slight numerical advantage. The convention devoted three days to debate on Articles II and III of the document, but the records, which are incomplete, disclose no comment on the question of a state's suability.[7] The delegates approved the Constitution by a narrow margin of 187 to 168, only after conciliatory recommendations for amendments were attached to the resolution of ratification. None of these touched upon the suability question, although one of them proposed an important limitation upon the diversity jurisdiction of the federal courts.[8]

Outside the convention, however, the suability question received attention. Sam Adams, whose general attitude as a delegate to the state convention was singularly ambivalent, is said to have manifested concern over the matter in his correspondence, and he subsequently reacted vigorously when the Supreme Court asserted jurisdiction in a case instituted against Massachusetts by a British subject.[9] Silas Lee, an emerging leader of the bar in Maine, feared that holders of state securities who were citizens of other states or foreign subjects would be able to sue the state for payment in the federal court.[10] James Sullivan, later to become attorney general of Massachusetts, also objected, but for other reasons.[11] He thought that extending judicial power to controversies between a state and citizens of other states and to diversity cases generally would entail very great inconvenience to the states. The individual, whether debtor, trespasser, or other under the laws of a particular state, might flee from his state, thereby putting it to great expense and trouble in proceeding against him, if, indeed, he did not evade trial altogether.

The most sustained misgivings regarding the judiciary article in general and the suability question in particular are revealed in letters by "Agrippa" published in the *Massachusetts Gazette* shortly before and during the state convention. These letters have been attributed to James Winthrop, the librarian at Harvard College.[12]

Initially Agrippa read the judiciary article as investing federal courts with authority "to try all causes between a state and its own citizens."[13]   While he thought that questions of property between such parties would be rare, the sovereignty of the states would be destroyed if they were forced to submit to litigation instituted by individuals. "The only case of the kind in which a state would probably be sued," he argued, "would be upon the state notes," and he saw endless confusion as the result of such suits.[14]   But this was only a secondary consideration for him. He was more fearful that the judiciary article would be construed to invest federal courts with jurisdiction over criminal cases instituted by the states. Thus the criminal defendant would be transported from the vicinage and tried among strangers.[15]

In later letters, Agrippa appears to have reinterpreted the judiciary article more restrictively. He ceased arguing that the jurisdiction of the federal courts would extend to cases between a state and its own citizens, but he maintained that the federal courts would have jurisdiction over both civil and criminal cases involving a state and citizens of other states. Consequently, the states would be liable to suit on state securities by such individuals, and where judgments against the state were rendered, both the public property of the state and the private property of the state's citizens would be liable to execution.[16]   Agrippa urged that the state convention reject the Constitution and then call for specific amendments to the Articles of Confederation. Among the amendments he proposed was one empowering Congress to "appoint courts, supreme and subordinate, with power to try all crimes, not relating to state securities, between any foreign country, or subject of such state, actually residing in a foreign country, and not being an absentee or person who has alienated himself from these states on the one part, and any of the United States or citizens thereof on the other part."[17]

Although some Massachusetts citizens criticized the judiciary article, others warmly defended it. The defenders saw the clauses

extending the judicial power of the United States to controversies
between a state and citizens of other states or foreign subjects as
conducive to justice between the parties. Such, for example, was
the view of Timothy Pickering, who commented in one of his
letters upon objections raised by the "Federal Farmer" and others
to this aspect of the federal judicial power.[18] Noting that the
states may pass laws that are unjust toward citizens of other states
and foreigners, Pickering thought it appropriate that these latter
have resort to an impartial federal forum. This, he implied, is
especially important in cases involving foreign nations and their
subjects, toward whom "this nation is responsible for the conduct
of all its members." The whole Union, he argued, might become
embroiled in war by the injustice of one state or one of its citizens
toward a foreign nation or subject, and for this reason the Union
should be empowered to dispense justice in such cases.

In the Virginia convention, like that in Massachusetts, Federalist
and anti-Federalist forces were closely balanced, although the
latter had an initial advantage. But in this convention, as in no
other, those opposed to ratification counted among their number
an array of talented and powerful advocates. For three weeks, the
delegates subjected the Constitution to a most thorough and
comprehensive scrutiny, and during this time debated the judiciary
article with unusual vehemence. Once again anti-Federalists feared
that the state judiciaries would be absorbed and that individual
liberty consequently would perish. They pressed their objections
to diversity jurisdiction and to the absence of a guarantee to trial
by jury in civil cases. And they warned that the judiciary article
made the state answerable to citizens of other states and to
foreigners in the federal courts—a charge which some Federalist
spokesmen denied but which others accepted.

Eight delegates discussed the question of the suability of a state
under the proposed Constitution. The issue seems to have been
raised initially by Edmund Randolph in an address before the
convention on June 10, 1788. In the course of his remarks in

support of ratification, Randolph professed his admiration for those parts of the Constitution prohibiting tender laws and impairments of the obligation of contracts and those forcing Virginia "to pay her debts." These provisions, virtually by themselves, seemed to warrant approval of the document, he argued.[19] Two days later Patrick Henry, in a forceful reply, went to the heart of the matter.[20] Arguing that the proposed Constitution made the states suable in federal court, Henry predicted that the holders of depreciated Continental paper and of other obligations would press for redemption at face value. Virginia, he said, may be required to pay her proportion of that currency, pound for pound. On June 17 Henry returned to the same theme: the state could be sued in federal court by northern holders of depreciated currency, who had purchased the notes for a tiny fraction of their face value. Moreover, the *ex post facto* and contract clauses precluded an equitable scaling of these obligations. The result would be financial ruin for the state and its citizens.[21]

George Nicholas, a proponent of ratification, replied to Henry with an unusual argument. The states, he thought, were suable, but Congress was not. And Congress alone was obligated to the individual holders of depreciated currency.[22] Edmund Pendleton, the president of the convention and a supporter of the Constitution, also defended the judiciary article. The federal judicial power, he said, reached only "cases of general and not local concern" and "the necessity and propriety of a federal jurisdiction, in all such cases, must strike every gentleman."[23]

Anti-Federalist objections were not abated by these arguments. On June 19, George Mason renewed the attack, arguing with considerable foresight that previous dispositions of western lands would be the source of claims instituted against the state in federal court.[24] Debts already paid, he contended, would have to be paid again if such power were vested in the federal judiciary. The state might be arraigned like a "delinquent individual, a culprit, or private offender" before a federal court. And to the clause extending the federal judicial power to controversies between a state and foreign states, Mason raised the further objection that there would be no reciprocity. How could a foreign state be bound by the decision? Would a state be entitled to sue a foreign state in tribunals of the latter? Mason then turned specifically to the claims of the Indiana Company, which, he accurately predicted, would be pressed in the federal courts.[25] In order to preclude such litigation, Mason submitted an amendment declaring that "the judicial power shall extend to no case where the cause of action shall have originated before the ratification of this Constitution, except in suits for debts due to the United States, disputes between states about their territory, and disputes between persons claiming lands under grants of different states."[26]

James Madison replied to Mason in a speech designed to allay the fears of anti-Federalists. Arguing that "it is not in the power of individuals to call any state into court," Madison stated that the challenged provision simply meant that if a state were to sue a citizen of another state, that suit must be brought in federal court.[27] To this interpretation of the clause, Patrick Henry professed astonishment and indignation. Indeed, he saw in Madison's explanation a dangerous tendency to "pervert the most clear expressions and the usual meaning of the language of the people." [28] The clause, he noted, made no distinction between plaintiffs and defendants. Neither reciprocity nor justice would be realized if Madison's interpretation were approved.[29]

In a reply to Henry, John Marshall reiterated the substance of Madison's argument. No state, he said, might be called before the bar of the federal court. The purpose of the clause was to enable states to recover claims from individuals residing in other states—a construction which he found "warranted by the words."[30] To the claim that this would be partial to the states, inasmuch as they could not be sued by individuals, he countered that it was inevitable.[31] But he noted that individuals might obtain redress by applying to the state legislatures.

Edmund Randolph made the last comment on the subject in the Virginia convention, and his statement indicates that the Madison-Marshall interpretation had not won unqualified approval from the Federalists, to say nothing of the anti-Federalists. Randolph viewed the clause as desirable because it rendered valid and effective existing claims against the state.[32]   And with respect to the western land claims, particularly that of the Indiana Company, he argued that the present settlers had clear legal title, but that the company could resort, under the Constitution, to the federal courts in order to obtain compensation from the state.[33]

In a resolution ratifying the Constitution, the Virginia convention proposed a bill of rights consisting of twenty articles and twenty amendments relating to other matters, but it refused to make the adoption of these amendments a condition of ratification.[34]   One of the amendments the Convention approved was based in part upon George Mason's proposal. The fourteenth article of amendment declared that the judicial power of the United States shall extend to "all cases in law and equity arising under treaties made, or which shall be made, under the authority of the United States; to all cases affecting ambassadors, other foreign ministers, and consuls; to all cases of admiralty and maritime jurisdiction; to controversies to which the United States shall be a party; to controversies between two or more states, and between parties claiming lands under the grants of different states."[35] This grant was made subject to the restriction that the federal judicial power would extend to no case, with certain specific exceptions, where the cause of action had originated prior to ratification of the Constitution. Under this proposal, a large part of the federal judicial power granted by the Constitution would have been substantially altered. Diversity jurisdiction would not have been given; the judicial power would not have extended to controversies between a state and citizens of other states and foreigners; cases arising under the Constitution and laws of the United States would have been withdrawn from federal cognizance. Such changes represented large concessions by supporters of ratification to win over wavering delegates, and even then the vote was extremely close.[36]

In New York, another state in which ratification was vital to the success of the new government, the story was much the same.[37] Here, too, Federalists appeared to be outnumbered by their opponents when the state convention met, but eventually they were successful by a thin margin and after concessions were made to the opposition.

Before the New York convention assembled, opponents of ratification raised the question of a state's suability under the judiciary article. The *Letters of a Federal Farmer,* written by Richard Henry Lee of Virginia, was published in New York and widely circulated there.[38]   Of the anti-Federalist tracts, this is generally regarded as having been most influential, both in Virginia and in New York. In discussing the judiciary article, Lee raised doubts as to the propriety of enabling a foreigner or citizen of another state to sue a state. The states, he noted, had defaulted upon many promises made during the war, and they had not been subject to suit for such delinquencies. Such remedies were not contemplated by either the states or their creditors at the time the contracts were made, and the "new remedy proposed to be given in the federal courts, can be founded on no principle whatever."[39]

Lee's objection apparently was widespread enough that Alexander Hamilton, in *The Federalist,* offered assurances.[40] Noting that some critics had suggested that the assignment of the public securities of one state to citizens of another state would enable the latter to sue the debtor state in federal court, Hamilton flatly denied that a sovereign could be sued by an individual without its consent. This exemption from suit, as an attribute of sovereignty, belonged to the states, and, unless surrendered in the Constitution, this immunity remained. Hamilton denied that the Constitution deprived the states of this sovereign attribute. The state governments would not be "divested of the privilege of paying their own debts in their own way, free from every constraint, but that which flows from the obligations of good faith."

The records of the New York convention do not disclose any discussion of the question of a state's suability, but it is certain that the matter occasioned concern. To the resolution ratifying the Constitution, which was approved 30 to 27, the convention appended numerous recommended amendments and declarations of understanding.[41] Among these was the following: "That the judicial power of the United States in cases in which a state may be a party, does not extend to criminal prosecutions, or *to authorize any suit by any person against a state.*"[42] The state convention then unanimously recommended that a second federal convention be called to make formal proposals of amendment.

New York was the eleventh state to ratify the Constitution, and its action assured the establishment of the new government. However, two states—North Carolina and Rhode Island—remained to be won over. In both, the paper-money faction had been either dominant or extraordinarily influential during the Confederation period, and consequently the issue of a state's suability under the Constitution was of considerable practical importance.

The North Carolina convention met for two weeks during the summer of 1788. By that time, Virginia had ratified the Constitution, and New York did so while the North Carolina convention was still in session. Despite these developments, anti-Federalist sentiment remained strong in North Carolina, and the convention, by a decisive vote, declined to ratify, although its action was not tantamount to outright rejection.

Anti-Federalist objections to the judiciary article, as revealed in convention proceedings, were, for the most part, quite general. But specific criticisms relating to the absence of a bill of rights and to the lack of a guarantee to trial by jury in civil cases were frequently voiced.[43] Only one Federalist delegate, William R. Davie, is recorded as having commented upon the clause extending the federal judicial power to controversies between a state and citizens of other states. He thought this provision "necessary to secure impartiality in decisions, and preserve tranquillity among the states,"[44] a view which was not, however, accepted by a majority of the convention delegates.

As a precondition to ratification, the convention insisted that a declaration of rights, together with amendments to the most ambiguous and exceptionable parts of the Constitution, be laid before Congress and a convention of states to be called to amend the document.[45] Among the twenty-six amendments, in addition to a bill of rights, that the North Carolina convention proposed was one delimiting the federal judicial power along the same lines as the amendment recommended by the Virginia convention, thereby withdrawing jurisdiction over controversies between a state and citizens of other states and foreigners.[46] Moreover, the convention proposed another amendment calculated to protect the state in its redemption of paper money: "That Congress shall not, directly or indirectly, either by themselves or through the judiciary, interfere with any one of the states in the redemption of paper money already emitted and now in circulation, or in liquidating and discharging the public securities of any one of the states, but each and every state shall have the exclusive right of making such laws and regulations, for the above purposes, as they shall think proper."[47] The resolution embodying these proposals of amendment and declining to ratify the Constitution was passed, 184 to 84. However, when a second state convention assembled the following year, after the establishment of the new federal government, it voted, 195 to 77, to ratify the Constitution.

In Rhode Island, opposition to ratification was even stronger. This state, whose policies were long dominated by the paper-money faction, had consistently refused to concur in amendments designed to strengthen the Confederation. It failed to send delegates to the Philadelphia Convention, and, when the Constitution was offered for ratification, the state legislature declined to call a state convention but submitted the document to a vote of the town meetings, where it was decisively rejected. But, in 1790, after the new government was already organized, and partly out of fear that the state would be treated as a foreign country by the United States, a convention was called. The minutes of its proceedings are sparse, and they do not reveal any discussion of the state suability issue; however, it is clear that the matter was not overlooked. Among the thirty-nine amendments proposed in the act of ratification was one declaring that "the judicial power of the United States, in cases in which a state may be a party, does not extend to criminal prosecutions, or to authorize any suit by any person against a state."[48] To further protect the state's financial and monetary policies, this proposed amendment specifically barred Congress and the judiciary from interfering with the states in the redemption of paper money and public securities.

From the foregoing review of the debates over ratification in various states, it should be evident that no uniform understanding was reached concerning the meaning of the clause extending the judicial power of the United States to "controversies between a state and citizens of another state." All of the anti-Federalists who commented upon the clause professed a belief that it made the states suable in federal court, and their adherence to this interpretation was not shaken by Federalist reassurances. In at least four states, delimiting or explanatory amendments were recommended by the conventions. Among the Federalists, opinion on the matter was sharply divided. On the one side were Edmund Randolph and James Wilson, who were members of the Committee of Detail where the clause originated. They interpreted the provision as making the states suable, while maintaining the intrinsic justice of establishing impartial tribunals for the disposition of such cases.

James Madison and Alexander Hamilton, who were delegates at Philadelphia, together with John Marshall, who was not, argued to the contrary that a state could not be sued by an individual except with its consent. While the importance of such statements should not be discounted altogether, there is little evidence that they were taken at face value by wavering delegates. In fact, these disclaimers probably attracted considerably more attention some years later after the Court had asserted jurisdiction over suits against the states than they received during the ratification debates.

On balance, the weight of expressed opinion seems to have been with those who believed, with either apprehension or satisfaction, that the states might be impleaded as defendants without their consent in suits instituted by citizens of other states and by foreign subjects in the federal courts. Whether the Constitution would have been ratified, in the absence of assurances that the states would not be suable, cannot be ascertained. But in any case, the legislative history of the Constitution hardly warrants the conclusion drawn by some that there was a general understanding, at the time of ratification, that the states would retain their sovereign immunity.

3

The States
Before the Court

With the ratification of the Constitution and the election of the First Congress, one of the first tasks confronting the new government was to organize the federal judiciary.[1] Article III, for the most part, was not self-executing; legislation was needed to fix the size of the Supreme Court, to create inferior federal courts, and to define the jurisdiction of these tribunals.

Legislative provision for the federal courts was made in the Judiciary Act of 1789, which Congress adopted after months of deliberation. The act was, in large measure, the handiwork of Oliver Ellsworth, who, as a member of the Committee of Detail of the Philadelphia Convention, had helped shape Article III. The First Congress, which deliberated upon and passed the act, was composed of many who had participated in framing and ratifying the Constitution. For these reasons, the Judiciary Act may be read as an important contemporaneous exposition of the original meaning attributed to Article III. But does the act disclose whether the clauses of that article concerning controversies between the states and specified parties were designed to relieve the states of their sovereign immunity?

Evidence is equivocal upon this point, but, on balance, it tends to support the hypothesis that the First Congress deemed the states to be suable by aliens and citizens of other states in the Supreme Court. Under Section 13 of the act, "the Supreme Court shall have jurisdiction of all controversies of a civil nature, where a state is a *party,* except between a state and its citizens; and except also between a state and citizens of other states, or aliens, in which latter case it shall have original but not exclusive jurisdiction."[2] This language does not go much beyond that used in the Constitution. It may be noteworthy that the Senate amended the committee's original bill to include the phrase, "except between a state and its citizens," but this matter will be considered later.[3] With respect to controversies between a state and citizens of other states or aliens, the statute, like Article III of the Constitution, refers to the states as a "party," without any differentiation between controversies in which a state is defendant and those in which it is plaintiff. In other words, if the quoted passage is read by itself, contradictory conclusions as to a state's immunity from suit may be inferred from it quite as readily as from the very similar language of Article III.

When the foregoing passage is compared, however, with other provisions of the Judiciary Act, the failure of Congress to differentiate between the states as plaintiffs and as defendants in controversies with noncitizens takes on considerable significance. In the very same section, Congress provided that the Supreme Court "shall have exclusively all such jurisdiction of suits or proceedings against ambassadors . . . *as a court can have or exercise consistently with the law of nations.* "[4] Here the immunity of diplomatic personnel, supposed to obtain under the Constitution, was nevertheless explicitly mentioned in the statute. The very same legislative caution is manifested in sections defining the jurisdiction of the inferior federal courts under the clause of Article III extending the judicial power to "controversies to which the United States shall be a party." In two different sections, Congress assigned jurisdiction over cases in which the United States was the plaintiff,[5] but no provision was made for jurisdiction over cases in which the United States was sued by an individual. It is difficult to account for these differences in textual treatment—as between controversies involving foreign diplomats and the United States, on the one hand, and those involving the states, on the other—unless the authors of the Judiciary Act in fact assumed that the states did not enjoy the immunity which the United States and foreign diplomats might claim.

Whatever may have been Congress' view, however, the Supreme Court almost immediately took cognizance of a suit in which a state was impleaded as the defendant. This case, *Vanstophorst* v. *Maryland,* was the very first to be docketed in the Supreme Court, and it was the precursor of other suits of this kind.[6] Indeed, during the Court's early years, before its appellate jurisdiction was fully engaged, its calendar was studded with a number of cases falling within its original jurisdiction; and suits instituted against various states by citizens of other states and by foreigners constituted an important part of the work load of the Court. In all, seven such suits involving six different states were filed prior to 1798, when ratification of the Eleventh Amendment was formally acknowledged. Two of these cases were not reported, and Dallas' reports of the others are fragmentary and inaccurate. However, the factual background of these cases, as well as the basic legal issues presented by them, can be pieced together from various sources.

Vanstophorst v. *Maryland* was a suit instituted at the February 1791 term of the Supreme Court by two Dutch financiers who had made large loans to the states and to Congress during and after the Revolutionary War. The plaintiffs sought recovery of principal, interest, and damages on a loan of £40,500 made to the state in 1782. Shortly after the loan was negotiated, the legislature of Maryland, believing the terms disadvantageous, annulled the contract and directed that the money be refunded. The refund, however, had not been made by the time the suit was instituted.[7]

Maryland did not resist compulsory process nor did it explicitly assent to the suit against it. The records disclose that a United States marshal, in the presence of two witnesses, served a summons upon the governor, the executive council, and the attorney general of the state; and the latter, Luther Martin, who was at the time a staunch defender of state sovereignty, directed John Caldwell to enter an appearance for the state.[8] Edmund Randolph, Attorney General of the United States, was retained as private counsel for the plaintiffs, and, on his motion, the Court ordered the state to enter a plea within two months, under penalty of a default judgment.

The case was carried over to the August 1791 term, when at the request of Randolph and with the consent of the defendant state, a commission was appointed to take depositions from certain witnesses residing in Holland.[9] Before the commission reported its findings, however, out-of-court negotiations looking toward a compromise settlement were undertaken, and, in 1792, the suit was discontinued on the motion of both the plaintiffs and defendants, each party agreeing to pay his own costs.[10]

Although the action of the Court, in asserting jurisdiction in this case, was full of important constitutional and political ramifications, it appears to have excited relatively little comment at the time, possibly because the defendant state failed to enter a formal protest.[11] Certainly the criticism which did occur was mild compared with that evoked when similar suits against the states of Georgia, Massachusetts, and Virginia were instituted a short time later. The *Vanstophorst* case, however, did occasion the publication of two unusually perceptive pamphlets, one by James Sullivan, attorney general of Massachusetts, challenging the Court's jurisdiction, and the other by Timothy Ford, who defended the Court's action.[12]

Even before the *Vanstophorst* case was withdrawn, a second suit was instituted in the Supreme Court against a state by an individual. This was *Oswald* v. *New York,* an action in *assumpsit* brought by the administrator of the estate of a Pennsylvania citizen.[13] In 1776, the New York convention appointed John Holt as state printer. Holt served in this capacity until his death in 1783, whereupon his widow was designated as printer by the state legislature. During his service, Holt does not appear to have been regularly paid, and, by the time of his death, the state owed him a substantial sum. A portion of this debt—consisting of charges for specific work—was paid to Holt's widow in 1786, but the state disallowed a claim for £1,383, a sum representing Holt's salary at the rate of £200 per year. This claim seems to have been rejected because the resolution appointing Holt and making provision for the salary was lost and because, in any event, the resolution could not have bound the state for more than one year.[14] It was upon the claim for £1,383 that *Oswald* v. *New York* was instituted.

This case, which caused the Court considerable embarrassment, first appeared on its February 1792 docket. At this time, a summons was directed to the defendant state, which declined to enter an appearance.[15] The plaintiff then moved for a *distringas* to compel the state to appear, but this request was subsequently withdrawn, and the suit was discontinued on plaintiff's motion. [16] During the August 1792 term of the Court, the suit was reinstated, however, when counsel for the plaintiff moved for "a rule on the marshal of the State of New York to return the writ issued against the said state."[17] The next day, the Court ordered "that the marshal of the New York district return the writ to him directed in this cause before the adjournment of this Court, if a copy of this rule shall be seasonably served upon him or his deputy—or otherwise on the first day of the next term. And that in case of default he do show cause therefor, by affidavit, taken before one of the Judges of the United States."[18] A return was made by the marshal at the February 1793 term, and, on motion of the plaintiff, the Court ordered that a default judgment against the state be entered at the next term unless the state appeared or showed cause for failure to do so. The case was continued with the plaintiff's consent, however, until the February 1795 term.

In the meantime, Governor George Clinton of New York

brought the matter to the attention of the state legislature.[19] On January 15, 1794, the state assembly, by a vote of 48 to 16, defeated a resolution, which, after reciting that the state had ratified the Constitution on the understanding that no suit could be instituted against a state by an individual, directed the attorney general to enter an appearance for the sole purpose of pleading to the jurisdiction of the court. "If such plea shall not be admitted, or shall be over-ruled, that then the said attorney general shall put in no plea relative to the merits of the said suit, or have any proceedings therein, which may be construed into an admission of the principle, that a suit may be brought in the said Court by any individual against this state."[20] A much milder resolution instructing the attorney general to defend the rights of the state was then passed, but even this resolution was not acceptable to the state senate. The upper chamber proposed a resolution instructing the attorney general to appear for the state and "make the best defense, the nature of the case will admit."[21] But the assembly defeated this resolution, as well as another calling for an amendment to the Constitution.[22]

During the February 1795 term of the Court, a jury was impaneled to hear the *Oswald* case.[23] An award, in the amount of $5,315 damages and $.06 costs, was rendered for the plaintiff; but the Court, still hesitating, entered judgment *nisi,* that is, a judgment to become effective unless the state appeared to contest it.[24] No appearance was subsequently entered, and there is no record indicating whether the state satisfied the judgment against it.

Even before judgment was entered in the *Oswald* case, three additional suits were instituted against states by citizens of other states and by aliens.[25] Criticism of the Court for asserting jurisdiction in *Vanstophorst* and *Oswald* had been restrained, but with these new suits political tempers began to flare. *Chisholm* v. *Georgia,* docketed in August 1792, became the most celebrated case of the pre-Marshall period.[26] It was the first case directly pitting the Court against a state government, and raised the perennial issue of state sovereignty under the Constitution. Despite the importance of the case, however, the facts of *Chisholm* v. *Georgia,* until recently, have been consistently misstated. They were not officially reported at the time, and a garbled newspaper account seems to have been the source of the traditional, but erroneous, view that the case was instituted in behalf of a British creditor and that it raised issues concerning the state's sequestration of Tory property.[27]

Actually, the case was brought by Alexander Chisholm, the executor of the estate of Robert Farquhar, a deceased South Carolina merchant from whom Georgia had purchased war supplies in 1777. The contract, which was negotiated by commissioners appointed by the state, called for payment of £63,605, South Carolina currency, on delivery of the merchandise. However, when delivery was made, Farquhar was not paid, although it appears that the state had issued continental loan office certificates to the commissioners for that purpose. Farquhar's efforts to obtain payment were unsuccessful during his lifetime, and, in 1789, the claim, then presented in behalf of his estate, was rejected by the Georgia legislature, which advised the claimant to sue the commissioners.[28]

Instead of suing the commissioners, who were insolvent, Chisholm brought suit against the state in the United States Circuit Court for the Georgia District.[29] This action for £100,000 sterling (principal, interest, and damages) was filed in 1790. Georgia responded promptly to the suit by asserting immunity and pleading to the jurisdiction of the court: "the state of Georgia cannot be drawn or compelled to answer against the will of the said State before any Justices of any Court of Law or Equity whatsoever."[30] In 1791, the circuit court, consisting of Supreme Court Justice James Iredell and District Judge Nathaniel Pendleton, sustained Georgia's challenge to the court's jurisdiction, and the suit was dismissed.

Chisholm persisted, however, by filing an original bill in the Supreme Court of the United States.[31] Attorney General Randolph was retained as counsel for the plaintiff. If personal dedication to a client's cause is a criterion for selection of counsel, a happier choice can scarcely be imagined. Randolph, it will be recalled, had participated in drafting the judiciary article. In the Virginia convention, he had pressed the view that the states were rightly made amenable to suits instituted by citizens of other states and by foreigners, and in the first case instituted against a state—*Vanstophorst* v. *Maryland*—Randolph had represented the plaintiffs.

Process was served upon the governor and attorney general of Georgia by a United States marshal. The defendant state failed to appear at the August 1792 term of the Court, and Randolph moved for a default judgment unless it appeared by the fourth day of the following term or showed cause for its failure to do so. With the consent of the plaintiff, consideration of this motion was postponed to February 1793.[32]

In a written protest, Georgia refused to enter an appearance,[33] and on February 5, 1793, the Court heard Randolph in support of the motion for a default judgment. The Attorney General began his argument by alluding to the rising chorus of criticism directed against him and the Court. "I did not want the remonstrance of Georgia, to satisfy me that the motion, which I have made is unpopular." Virginia, too, he noted, had condemned the motion, and such expressions ordinarily would have influenced him greatly. But where "a constitutional right, supported by my own conviction" is brought into question, surrender would be "official perfidy."[34] Randolph proceeded to consider four questions to which the Court had specifically directed his attention.

The first of these questions was whether Georgia could be made a defendant in a suit instituted in the Supreme Court of the United States by a citizen of another state. In replying to this question, Randolph reviewed the provisions of the Constitution and the Judiciary Act. A literal construction of either instrument, he argued, yielded an affirmative answer. And this conclusion was buttressed by an analysis of the spirit of the Constitution. In numerous particulars, he maintained, the Constitution imposed restrictions upon the states; obvious examples were the prohibitions against *ex post facto* laws, bills of attainder, laws impairing contractual obligations, and the emission of bills of credit. Randolph conceded that there were remedies other than suit against a state for violations of these prohibitions. Thus, a convict held under an *ex post facto* law or bill of attainder might be ordered discharged. The sanctity of contractual obligations might be defended. But, he added, such redress was incomplete because "some of the preceding unconstitutional actions must pass without censure unless states can be made defendants." The estate of a citizen might be confiscated by an *ex post facto* law and deposited into the public treasury or a state might adulterate the coin, emit bills of credit, enact tender laws, or impair its own contracts. Such evils, he asserted, could not be corrected without suit against the state by the aggrieved party.[35]

In support of the conclusion that the states were suable by citizens of other states and by foreigners, Randolph discussed the relations between the state and federal governments. While acknowledging that the states were sovereignties, he argued that with "free will, arising from absolute independence" they combined to form a "government for their own happiness." First the confederation, which "cried aloud for its own reform," was established, and subsequently the Constitution, which "derives its origins immediately from the people," was adopted. The people made themselves individually subject to restraints, and the states, as assemblages of people, were liable to legal process, with corresponding diminution of their sovereignty. From this, he reasoned that "there is nothing in the nature of sovereignties, combined as those in America are, to prevent the words of the constitution, from receiving an easy and usual construction."[36] Randolph then suggested the consequences of immunizing a state from suit by citizens of other states and by foreigners. The result, he said, would be the disruption of domestic tranquillity and international peace, the maintenance of which was a primary object of the Constitution.[37]

The Attorney General turned to what he described as the "master objection" to the amenability of states to suits by individuals—the want of explicit power in the judiciary to execute process against them. To this objection, he responded that the Judiciary Act of 1789 prescribed certain writs and left the formulation of others to the discretion of the Court.[38] If there was no specific provision for writs in cases instituted by an individual against a state, neither was there such provision in cases instituted by a state against another state; and clearly this did not derogate from the Court's jurisdiction with respect to controversies between states.

To the remaining questions propounded by the Court, Randolph gave brief answer.[39] He thought that an *assumpsit* was clearly a cause that would lie against a state, for a state is capable of making a promise. Service of process upon the governor was, he argued, competent, because the governor was the ostensible representative of the state. Finally, as to the steps appropriate for compelling appearance by the state, he suggested that these might be devised by the Court as occasion warranted.

When Randolph concluded his presentation, the Court noted that "no appearance had been entered on the part of the state of Georgia and regarding the question involved in the suit as highly important suggest to the counsellors of the Court that if any are disposed to offer their sentiments on the subject now under consideration the Court are willing to hear them."[40] No member of the bar volunteered, and the Court took the case under advisement.

Thirteen days later, on February 18, the five participating justices announced their opinions,[41] and judgment on Randolph's motion was rendered. The composition of the Court is of some interest, for all members had figured more or less prominently in events leading up to the establishment of the new government. Two of the justices—James Wilson of Pennsylvania and John Blair of Virginia—had been delegates to the Federal Convention, and Wilson had served, with great brilliance, as the leading Federalist spokesman in the Pennsylvania convention. William Cushing of

Massachusetts, James Iredell of North Carolina, and Chief Justice Jay of New York had been members of the conventions of their respective states; moreover, both Jay and Iredell had authored widely circulated essays in support of ratification.

In accordance with the existing practice of delivering opinions *in seriatim,* each member spoke separately, after which the judgment of the Court was announced. Justice Iredell, the lone dissenter, was the first to speak. In an elaborate, learned opinion focusing upon a relatively narrow issue, Iredell maintained that the Court had no jurisdiction in the case. For him, the question to be considered was not whether a state, under any circumstances, might be made a defendant over its objection in a suit brought by a citizen of another state. Rather it was whether an action of *assumpsit* might be instituted against a state by an individual. He conceded, however, that "everything I have to say will affect every kind of suit, the object of which is to compel the payment of money by a state."[42]

Although Justice Iredell discussed the matter of sovereignty and its locus under Constitution in orthodox Federalist terms, the main emphasis of his opinion was on a much narrower question: did the Court derive jurisdiction directly from the Constitution and independently of any statute? This he answered negatively. Furthermore, he saw nothing in the Judiciary Act to indicate that Congress had granted jurisdiction over cases of the kind before the Court.[43] Up to this point, the dissenting opinion was a model of self-restraint, but, in concluding, Iredell indicated that if Congress attempted to authorize suits such as this, the jurisdiction would not be warranted by the Constitution.[44]

The principal opinions supporting the Court's jurisdiction were delivered by Justice Wilson and Chief Justice Jay. Justices Blair and Cushing authored relatively brief opinions, emphasizing a literal reading of the judiciary article.

The Wilson opinion, written in the expansive language of the time, is justly famed as a grandiloquent judicial exposition of general constitutional doctrines. The concepts of popular sovereignty and national supremacy defended so well in that opinion were, of course, essential components in the doctrinal development of judical nationalism set forth by John Marshall a few years later. But perhaps because Wilson seized upon *Chisholm* v. *Georgia* as a medium for expounding a strongly nationalist constitutional philosophy, his opinion is rather weak in certain technical particulars. Moreover, as a state paper, it was at least impolitic; many contemporary statesmen and politicians read it as an exercise in judicial usurpation, which called for repudiation.

For Wilson, the transcendent issue was whether "the people of the United States form a nation,"[45] which he proposed to answer by examining principles of general jurisprudence, the laws and practices of particular nations, and the Constitution of the United States. In fact, much of his argument is based upon natural-rights philosophy. Man alone, Wilson argued, is the work of a perfect creator; the state is a contrivance of man, thus inferior to man but superior to all else, including government. By state, he meant "a complete body of free persons united together for their common benefit, to enjoy peaceably what is their own, and to do justice to others."[46] The state has rules, rights, and obligations; it may incur debts and bind itself by contract. And general principles of justice are as binding upon the state as upon the individual person. If law may bind one man, it may bind men in the aggregate.

Wilson rejected the claim that the states were sovereign in the sense that they were immune from legal process. He associated this claim with recent despotic tendencies introduced in England, and he sought to counter the idea by resorting to general principles of jurisprudence and to some precedents elsewhere.[47] In these precedents, shadowy though they were, Wilson professed to see much in favor of the Court's jurisdiction over the state of Georgia.

In the last part of his opinion, Wilson examined the Court's jurisdiction under the Constitution. His argument is an eloquent defense of national supremacy based upon the will of the sovereign people. As the people were competent to alter the power of the states, they could invest the federal courts with jurisdiction over the states. Wilson concluded that both the letter and the general principles of the Constitution supported the jurisdiction.

Chief Justice Jay closely seconded most of Wilson's sentiments. In replying to the claim that the state was immune from suit, Jay posed three questions: (1) In what sense is a state sovereign? (2) Is suability compatible with state sovereignty? (3) Did the Constitution authorize an action of the kind involved here?[48]

To answer the first question, the Chief Justice invoked what was eventually to become standard lawyers' history. Prior to the American Revolution, sovereignty resided in the British crown, and, with the Declaration of Independence, this sovereignty passed to the people, who, for national purposes, considered themselves one people. When the Articles of Confederation proved disappointing to them, the people established a new Constitution. This Constitution was a compact whereby the people agreed among themselves to be governed in a certain manner, and this compact transferred many prerogatives from the state governments to the national government.[49] In Europe different principles, based upon the feudal system, prevailed. There the prince was sovereign—the fountain of justice—and this excluded the idea that ruler and subject were equal. In the United States, however, sovereignty of the nation was in the people of the nation, and the "residuary sovereignty" of each state was in the people thereof.

Proceeding to the second question, Chief Justice Jay maintained that the sovereignty of Georgia, insofar as such existed, was not incompatible with the suability of the state. A free citizen, he noted, may sue another; a citizen may sue a municipality; and a citizen may sue a state. There was no rational basis for granting the citizens of the state of Delaware an immunity from suit denied to the citizens of the city of Philadelphia. Moreover, it was beyond argument that a state was suable in the Supreme Court at the instance of another state, and this fact alone meant that state sovereignty and immunity from suit were not inseparable. It was also clear that a state may sue a citizen of another state, as, indeed, Georgia had already done.[50] The rule should work both ways.

In the concluding paragraphs of his opinion, Chief Justice Jay examined the judicial power conferred by the Constitution. The people sought to remedy earlier defects of government, and the preamble to the Constitution made explicit the objectives of the people. As interpreted by the Chief Justice, the various extensions of federal judicial power were designed to fulfill some of these objectives. With respect to cases between a state and citizens of other states, he commented:

> because in case a state (that is, all the citizens of it) has demands against some citizens of another state, it is better that she should prosecute their demands in a national court, than in a court of the state to which those citizens belong; the danger of irritation and criminations arising from apprehensions and suspicions of partiality, being thereby obviated. Because, in cases where some citizens of one state have demands against all the citizens of another state, the cause of liberty and the rights of men forbid, that the latter should be the sole judges of the justice due to the latter; and true republican government requires that free and equal citizens should have free, fair, and equal justice.[51]

To the contention that the clause conferring judicial power over controversies between a state and citizens of other states should be construed as permitting only a state to sue, Jay responded that the power was remedial, and consequently it should be liberally interpreted. Neither the language nor the spirit of the Constitution demanded such a restrictive construction:

> The exception contended for, would contravene and do violence to the great and leading principles of a free and equal national government, one of the great objects of which is, to ensure justice to all. It would be strange, indeed, that the joint and equal sovereigns of this country, should, in the very Constitution by which they professed to establish justice, so far deviate from the plain path of equality and impartiality, as to give to the collective citizens of one state, a right

of suing individual citizens of another state, and yet deny to those citizens a right of suing them.[52]

In pursuing this last line of argument Chief Justice Jay was disturbed by one consideration. Article III extended the federal judicial power to "controversies to which the United States shall be a party." The word "party," he thought, might be defined as encompassing both plaintiff and defendant status. Could, then, the United States, like a state, be sued? To this question Jay suggested, albeit equivocally, a negative answer, because he perceived a difference of circumstances. In actions against the states or individuals, national courts were supported in their judgments by the national executive, but there was no higher executive arm to which the courts could turn for enforcement of a decree against the United States. He expressed the hope, however, that in time the whole nation might be compelled to do justice according to law at the suit of an individual.

The decree of the Court directed that the plaintiff file his declaration on or before March 1, providing it be served on the governor and attorney general of Georgia. A default judgment was to be entered if the state did not appear by the first day of the next term, but there were further delays. In February 1794, judgment was finally entered against the state, and a writ of inquiry for damages was awarded at that time.[53] The writ, however, was not executed, probably because the Farquhar claim was settled by the state later that year.[54] Still, the case of *Chisholm* v. *Georgia* remained on the Court's docket until 1798, when it was dismissed in *Hollingsworth* v. *Virginia*.

In the meantime, resentment against the *Chisholm* decision was running high, and reaction came swiftly, in Georgia and elsewhere.[55] When the legislature of Georgia convened in the autumn of 1793, Governor Edward Telfair presented the matter formally at a joint session. Noting that the Constitution had already been amended in several particulars, the Governor asserted that the state legislatures had continuing responsibility to propose amendments that would make that document more definite. He had declined to enter an appearance in *Chisholm* because "this would have introduced a precedent replete with danger to the republic."[56] The retained sovereignty of the state would have been impaired, and there would have been serious practical consequences as well. Even the political existence of the state would be annihilated if actions to recover on paper money emitted by the state were admissible. To guard against "civil discord and the impending danger," Governor Telfair urged the legislature to adopt a measure directing Georgia's delegation in Congress to seek a constitutional amendment and calling upon the legislatures of the other states to ratify such an amendment once it was proposed. In response to these remarks a committee of the state house of representatives recommended that (1) the legislature enact a bill declaratory of the state's retained sovereignty, (2) the legislature address the legislatures of the other states requesting their concurrence in an explanatory amendment to the Constitution, and (3) the governor transmit the proceedings urging this amendment to the state's senators and representatives in Congress. These recommendations were adopted, and the committee was instructed to bring in a bill and an address.[57]

Georgia's legislative records contain sparse information on subsequent proceedings. The lower house considered the special committee's bill in committee of the whole and voted several amendments. Manifesting the intensity of feeling which characterized the debates, the house refused to delete, by a vote of 19 to 8, the following section:

> That any Federal Marshal, or any other person or persons levying or attempting to levy on the territory of this state or any part thereof, or on the treasury or any other property of the Governor or Attorney General, or any of the people thereof, under or by virtue of any execution or other compulsory process issuing out of, or by authority of the supreme court of the United States, as it now stands, be constituted; for, or in behalf of the before-mentioned Alexander Chisholm, executor of Robert Farquhar, or for, or in

behalf of any other person or persons whatsoever, for the payment or recovery of any debt or pretended debt, or claim against the said state of Georgia; shall be, and or they attempting to levy as aforesaid, are hereby declared to be guilty of felony, and shall suffer death, without the benefit of the clergy, by being hanged.[58]

The state senate did not agree to the bill, however—possibly because of developments pointing to eventual reversal of the Court's holding by constitutional amendment.

It may be conjectured that the opposition to the Court engendered by the *Chisholm* decree would have dissipated in time without yielding concrete results if the "sovereignty" of Georgia had been the sole issue. The history of the Supreme Court is replete with specific decisions having both immediate incidence upon particular states and wide import for "states' rights." Although such decisions normally evoke intense local, and occasionally sectional, opposition, the reaction of states not immediately and practically affected has often been disappointing to those that are. Such might have been the situation here, had not the Court already taken cognizance of similar cases involving other states. On the day following the *Chisholm* decision, the Court entered a default judgment against New York in the *Oswald* case, and, as we have already seen, this judgment eventuated in a jury verdict awarding damages to the plaintiff. Litigation threatening the most serious practical consequences had already been instituted, or was immediately impending, against Virginia and Massachusetts. Moreover, before ratification of the Eleventh Amendment was formally acknowledged, another suit against Georgia began, and a judgment against South Carolina was rendered.[59]

In *Grayson* v. *Virginia*[60] the dire prophecies of anti-Federalists in the Virginia convention seemed destined to materialize. This case, variously entitled *Hollingsworth* v. *Virginia* and *Indiana Company* v. *Virginia*,[61] was a suit in equity brought by some ninety persons, most of them citizens of Pennsylvania and all of them shareholders in the Indiana Company. In 1768, while Virginia was a British colony, several Indian tribes conveyed approximately three million acres of land to a group of fur traders as reparation for having seized and carried off property valued at nearly a quarter million dollars. Although the British government approved this transaction, the Virginia legislature in 1779 declared the conveyance to be void and claimed the land as part of the public domain. Subsequent legislation provided for the establishment of local governmental units within the tract, and the state land office was authorized to sell the land, with receipts accruing to the state. The shareholders repeatedly petitioned the state legislature for redress, but without success. The Confederation Congress adopted a resolution asking the state to desist from further sales, but it ignored this request. Against this background, the suit was commenced in the Supreme Court in August 1792, when plaintiffs filed a bill in equity asking relief either in the sum of $1,128,000 (the estimated sale value of the land) or in the amount of $233,000 (the value of the property seized by the Indians).[62]

Even before the suit was formally instituted, plans to combat the action were under consideration by the state of Virginia.[63] And, shortly after the litigation began, the state legislature approved a resolution denying that the Court possessed any jurisdiction in the case and declaring sweepingly that "the state cannot be made a defendant in the said court, at the suit of any individual or individuals." By this resolution the state executive was requested "to pursue such measures as it may deem conducive to the interest, honor, and dignity of this commonwealth."[64] Attorney General James Innes described the dilemma confronting the state executive in a letter to Governor Henry Lee.[65] Lamenting that the resolutions of the state legislature did not prescribe the strategy of the state, Innes noted that if counsel were not employed, the jurisdictional issues would not be raised and the Indiana Company's bill might be treated as having been conceded by the state. If, however, the state did appear, its action might be interpreted as an acknowledgment of the Supreme Court's power "to cite her before its tribunal." As to the proper course, the attorney general was unable to offer definite advice. Perhaps, he thought, a member of the executive department should go to Philadelphia with authority to adopt whatever measures may be proper "to preserve the sovereignty of the state from the attempted usurpations." In response to this suggestion, Governor Lee went to Philadelphia, where he was present at the time of the Court's decision in the *Chisholm* case. In a letter to Lieutenant Governor James Wood, he predicted that a judgment in favor of the Indiana Company would be rendered at the next term of the Court if Virginia followed the example of Georgia and failed to enter an appearance. He also stated that he had suggested to the state's congressional delegation the propriety of an explanatory constitutional amendment concerning the federal judicial power.[66]

The Court's decision in *Chisholm* thoroughly aroused the legislature of Virginia to the impending danger. The state's claims to the Indiana tract were at best cloudy, and the amount of the relief the Indiana claimants sought was considerable. Moreover, the state feared that successful litigation by the Indiana claimants would revive old questions about the state's disposition of other land claims, principally those of the late Judge Richard Henderson, who had attempted unsuccessfully to create the proprietary state of Transylvania in the Cumberland region of Kentucky, then a part of Virginia.[67] Late in 1793 the legislature passed two resolutions bearing upon the *Chisholm* decision and the pending suit against Virginia. The first of these declared that the Court's decision in *Chisholm* "is incompatible with and dangerous to the sovereignty of the individual states, as the same tends to a general consolidation of these confederated republics." The second instructed the state's senators and requested its representatives to unite with those of other states in obtaining clarifying amendments to the Constitution.[68] These resolutions were adopted unanimously by the lower chamber, and they encountered only token opposition in the state senate.

Throughout 1794 and 1795, the Indiana litigation continued; neither the plaintiffs nor the Court, in light of the furor created by the *Chisholm* case, seemed disposed to press for an early judgment. In 1796, however, the plaintiffs moved for a *distringas* to compel the appearance of the state.[69] The Court delayed action on this motion, but during the August 1796 term it announced new rules designed to relieve some of the embarrassments attendant upon the issuance of process against a state. Under these rules, the Court ordered "that when process at common law or in equity shall issue against a state, the same shall be served on the governor and attorney general of such state."[70] The other order permitted complainants to proceed *ex parte* where, after sixty days following service of a subpoena upon the defendant, the latter failed to enter an appearance. The Indiana claimants then withdrew the motion for a *distringas,* and the Court, at their request, granted an alias subpoena. In 1797 the Court granted rules for commissions to examine witnesses, and the case was continued through the summer term. Meanwhile, ratification of the Eleventh Amendment was finally acknowledged, and in February 1798 the Court dismissed the suit, together with others, in *Hollingsworth* v. *Virginia.*[71]

Another case in which a state was impleaded before the Supreme Court by an individual was docketed before Congress proposed the Eleventh Amendment. This was *Vassall* v. *Massachusetts,* begun only a few months after the Court's disposition of the jurisdictional issue in *Chisholm.*[72] Here the substantive claim of the plaintiff—a Loyalist who had fled to England during the war—turned on the validity of the state's confiscation of absentee properties. Potentially most of the states would have been affected by judicial recognition of Vassall's claim, and practical and symbolic consequences of the greatest importance would ensue.

When, during the summer of 1793, a federal marshal made service upon Governor Hancock and Attorney General Sullivan, the state executive reacted quickly to the challenge, issuing a proclamation calling the legislature into special session in September. Although critically ill and too weak to stand, Hancock made a dramatic appearance before a joint session, and in his presence the

secretary of the commonwealth read the governor's message.[73] On
the whole, his remarks were surprisingly moderate in tone. Declaring that he could not conceive that the people of the commonwealth, in adopting the Constitution, "expected that each state
should be held to answer, on compulsory civil process, to every
individual resident in another state or in a foreign kingdom," the
governor stated that he was not authorized to enter an appearance
in any court without first consulting the legislature.[74] Vassall's
demand, he noted, turned on the legality of the state's absentee
laws—a matter "which may greatly inspire the interest and dis-
agreeably affect the feelings of the citizens of this commonwealth."[75] Hancock saw several alternatives which the legislature
might pursue. If it agreed that the state was liable to be sued, it
should make provision for defense against the action. But, if the
legislature thought the state immune from such an action, it
should seek a more favorable construction of the judiciary article.
Finally, the legislature might consider the state liable according to
the letter of the Constitution, yet, in the interest of peace and
harmony, it could decide to seek an amendment to the judiciary
article.

The governor declined to give a definite opinion on the general
amenability of the state to suit by an individual in the federal
courts, but it is clear that he regarded it as limited. There should
be, he argued, a tribunal independent of the several states in order
to preserve the peace and safety of the Union and to establish the
confidence of foreign nations in the rectitude of the United States.
But he doubted that the judicial power of the United States
extended to matters of civil contract involving the states. It might
more properly be confined to other matters—to providing a
remedy for "such injuries as may take place by force," which tend
to destroy domestic peace and to involve the nation in foreign
wars.[76] In such cases, the law of nations, the Constitution, and
treaties provide the law for a judicial judgment. If, however, the
judicial power extended to suits against the states on civil con-

tracts, what law would be applicable? It would be absurd, Hancock argued, to apply either the law of the state that is sued or that of the state or kingdom to which the claimant belonged. And if the law to be applied were that of the United States, this "would render the legislative authority of Congress over the particular states, as mere corporations commensurate to the claim of the judiciary power."

The legislature promptly responded to Governor Hancock's address by voting a resolution declaring that the power of compelling a state to be made a defendant in any federal court at the suit of an individual was "unnecessary and inexpedient, and in its exercise, dangerous to the peace, safety, and independence of the several states and repugnant to the first principles of a federal government."[77] The senators from the state were instructed and the representatives admonished to seek amendments to the Constitution, and the governor was requested to communicate the resolution to the legislatures of the other states.

With action now imminent in Congress, the subsequent judicial history of *Vassall* v. *Massachusetts* was somewhat anticlimactic. There is no record of the state's appearance. Neither the plaintiff nor the Court pressed for an early decision in the case, and, at successive terms of the Court, continuances were repeatedly granted until February 1797, when the case was dismissed.[78]

One other state, South Carolina, was sued by a noncitizen in the Supreme Court of the United States. In *Cutting* v. *South Carolina,* an unreported case, the executor of the Prince of Luxembourg brought suit in equity to recover a debt owed by South Carolina on the account of a vessel owned by the state.[79] The state acknowledged its indebtedness, but withheld payment because the French Republic claimed that it had succeeded to the obligation.

In February 1796, counsel for the plaintiff moved for a return of process by the beginning of the August term of the Court. Service was attempted upon the governor of South Carolina by a United States marshal, but the governor declined to accept the writ. In a message to the legislature, the governor justified his refusal to accept process upon the ground that "it was derogatory to the credit and honor of the state to permit a suit to be brought against it for a debt which was liquidated and acknowledged by it, and which the state declined paying only on account of a claim which had been made on behalf of the French Republic."[80]

After the state failed to appear, the Supreme Court entered a default judgment in February 1797. In August, a jury was impaneled to "enquire what damages the plaintiff sustained by reason of the nonperformance of certain promises set forth in his declaration," and the plaintiff proceeded *ex parte*. The jury subsequently returned a verdict in the amount of $55,002 for the plaintiff.[81] South Carolina immediately brought suit to stay execution of the judgment, and an injunction was awarded upon the condition that the state deposit in Court the amount of the judgment. It is not clear whether the state satisfied this condition, but there is no record that a writ of execution issued.

In February 1798, following its decree in *Hollingsworth* v. *Virginia,* the Court, with the consent of the parties, directed a continuance of *Cutting* v. *South Carolina.* Other cases in which states had been sued by individuals were at the time dismissed upon the basis of the Eleventh Amendment. Perhaps the *Cutting* case was not dismissed because the Eleventh Amendment did not, by its terms, preclude actions instituted by a foreign state or sovereign against a nonconsenting state.[82] The later record is silent as to the ultimate disposition of the case.

One other case completes the roster of suits instituted against a state in the Supreme Court of the United States before 1798, when the Eleventh Amendment was officially proclaimed. This was *Moultrie* v. *Georgia,* otherwise entitled *Huger* v. *Georgia,* a bill in equity filed in February 1797 by the shareholders of the South Carolina Yazoo Company.[83] In 1789, the Georgia legislature agreed to sell to three land companies nearly 16 million acres of western lands claimed by the state. The total purchase price, to be paid within two years, was $200,000, of which the South Carolina Company was to pay a little more than one-third. However, in 1790, before the purchase price was tendered, the legislature passed a resolution requiring payment in specie. The company by this time was in financial difficulty and unable to meet the requirement, and the state treasurer refused to accept paper money or other certificates in satisfaction of the price. In 1795 the Georgie legislature, treating the contract as no longer binding upon it, sold a part of the tract to other parties, who in turn conveyed to the New England Company.[84] In the complaint filed in the Supreme Court, shareholders of the South Carolina Company alleged that the state, in requiring payment in specie and refusing tender of paper, had breached the original contract of sale, and they asked for a decree confirming their title against the state and its subsequent grantees. A subpoena was served upon the attorney general of the state, but the action came to nothing when, the following year, the Court held that the Eleventh Amendment barred pending, as well as future, suits against a state by citizens of other states and by aliens.

The Court's holding in *Chisholm* v. *Georgia* and its assertion of jurisdiction over other suits against states brought renewed efforts to circumscribe the federal judicial power by constitutional amendment. At the time of ratifying the Constitution, four states—Virginia, New York, North Carolina, and Rhode Island— had urged amendments depriving the federal judiciary of the power to decide cases instituted against a state by a citizen of another state or by an alien. And after the adoption of the Constitution, but prior to the *Chisholm* decision, at least one proposed amendment to this effect was introduced in the House of Representatives, which declined to act on it.[85]

Congressional reaction to *Chisholm* came quickly. Only two days after the decree was announced, a resolution, of uncertain authorship, proposing the following amendment was introduced in the Senate:

> The Judicial power of the United States shall not extend to any suits in law or equity, commenced or prosecuted against one of the United States by citizens of another State, or by citizens or subjects of any foreign State.[86]

This resolution was debated on February 25, 1793, but the Second Congress adjourned in early March without taking any action on the matter.

When the Third Congress assembled in December 1793, the fears and antagonisms created by the *Chisholm* case and other pending suits were being fully aired. Massachusetts and Virginia, both of which had been involuntarily impleaded in suits by noncitizens, were the first to act, with resolutions strongly condemning the Court's action. The legislatures of both states resorted to the familiar practice of directing that their resolutions be transmitted to the executives and legislatures of other states. And, during the fall and winter of 1793, virtually every state governor referred to *Chisholm* and the Massachusetts and Virginia resolutions in messages to their respective legislatures. The legislatures of North Carolina and Connecticut formally responded with resolutions critical of the Court's decision.[87] A joint session of the New Hampshire legislature voted a similar resolution, which was not formally adopted because the two houses did not act separately upon it.[88] And in the New York, Maryland, South Carolina, and Georgia legislatures, official action was prevented by deadlocks between the legislative houses on the wording of their resolutions.[89] A committee of the Pennsylvania House of Representatives urged the propriety of a constitutional amendment, but the committee report was not approved.[90] There were, on the other hand, a few expressions in favor of the Court's decision. A committee of the Delaware Senate, for example, commented that justice, probity, and good faith made it improper to exempt the states from suit. Groups of people, whether associated as companies, corporations, or states, should be "as compellable to pay their debts as individuals are," and the means for obtaining justice should be as certain in the one case as in the other.[91]   The legislature, however, adjourned without acting upon the commit-tee report.

The resolution proposing the exact text of the Eleventh Amend-ment was introduced in the United States Senate on January 2, 1794:

> The Judicial power of the United States shall not be construed to extend to any suit in law or equity, commenced or prosecuted against one of the United States by citizens of another State, or by citizens or subjects of a foreign State.[92]

It may be noted that in one respect this proposal differed from the amendment introduced in the previous Congress. The words "be construed to" were inserted, a change which some commentators have interpreted as indicating that the amendment was declaratory of a general understanding which the Court had traduced in asserting jurisdiction over suits of this kind.

Consideration of the resolution was postponed until January 13, and debate, which was not reported, continued into the following day. A substitute proposed by Senator Albert Gallatin of Pennsylvania was defeated:

> The Judicial power of the United States, except in cases arising under treaties made under the authority of the United States, shall not be construed to extend to any suit in law or equity, commenced or prosecuted against one of the United States, by citizens of another State, where the cause of action shall have arisen before the ratification of this amendment.[93]

The Senate then passed, 23 to 2, the original resolution.

On January 15, 1794, the House of Representatives received the Senate message transmitting the resolution and requesting the concurrence of the lower chamber. Consideration was deferred until March 4, when an effort was made to restrict the application of the amendment by adding the words "where such State shall have previously made provision in their own courts, whereby such suit may be prosecuted to effect."[94] This modification was defeated, 77 to 8, and the resolution proposing the Eleventh Amendment passed, 81 to 9.

When the amendment was proposed by Congress, there were fifteen states in the Union. Therefore, the approval of twelve states was at that time necessary for ratification. The response was swift and decisive. The first state to ratify was New York, within a month after Congress proposed the amendment.[95] By February 1795, eleven other states appear to have acted affirmatively, completing the ratification process.[96] Token opposition was expressed in most of the legislatures; in only Maryland was the vote close.[97] Pennsylvania and New Jersey refused to ratify, while the South Carolina legislature deferred action for unascertained reasons.

Certification of action by the ratifying states was extremely erratic, however, and for this reason the amendment was not immediately recognized as a part of the Constitution. By January 1796—a year after the requisite number of state legislatures had assented—President Washington had transmitted to Congress notices of ratification by only eight states. The following year Congress voted a resolution requesting President Adams to ascertain whether favorable action had been taken in other states, including Tennessee, which had recently been admitted as the sixteenth state. Early in 1798 Adams notified Congress that twelve states had ratified and that the amendment was now effective.[98] Actually, by this time, South Carolina had become the thirteenth state to vote approval, and in the end only Pennsylvania, New Jersey, and Tennessee failed to act favorably.[99]

Two explanations generally have been offered for the widespread support which the Eleventh Amendment attracted in Congress and in the state legislatures. Some have contended that the amendment simply reaffirmed a general understanding existing at the time the Constitution was ratified. [100] According to this view, the amendment encountered little opposition because there was broad agreement among those who framed and ratified the Constitution that the states were to be immune from suit by individuals, in spite of the clauses of Article III extending the federal judicial power to controversies "between a State and Citizens of another State . . . and between a State . . . and foreign States, Citizens or Subjects." Others have suggested that the amendment won easy approval because the states were fearful that they would be compelled by the Supreme Court to pay certain debts, specifically obligations owing, or subsequently assigned, to noncitizen creditors. [101]

Each of those explanations for the amendment's success is related to some purpose thought to be implicit in the amendment. They are not, of course, mutually exclusive, but whether taken separately or together, they do not provide a full or accurate account of why the amendment enlisted widespread support.

Both the debates on ratification of the Constitution and the text of the Eleventh Amendment have been cited to support the conclusion that the amendment's sponsors saw it as simply restoring the limits of Article III as originally understood by those who framed and ratified the Constitution. The ratification debates, however, as we have already seen, do not indicate any general understanding that the states were to retain their sovereign immunity, although some delegates did interpret Article III in that way. Moreover, inferences drawn from the text of the amendment are inconclusive. While it is plausible to infer from insertion of the words "be construed to" in the final version of the amendment that it was intended to correct an erroneous judicial interpretation, other inferences are possible. The words may have been added as a gesture toward those state legislatures that, in the wake of *Chisholm,* had called for an explanatory amendment. Or they may have been inserted as a way to ensure retrospective application of the amendment to suits already filed. Finally, in inserting these words, Congress may have sought to soften any supposed rebuke to the Court, by indicating that the Court's interpretation of Article III allowing suits against the states, while tenable, was to be abandoned in favor of the opposite construction.

The second explanation—that the Eleventh Amendment attracted general support because the states were fearful that they would be required to pay debts owing to noncitizens—appears to be even more doubtful than the first. While the extension of the federal judicial power to controversies between a state and noncitizens very well may have been intended to afford a means for recovery on debts owed by the state, it does not follow that the Eleventh Amendment, in barring such judicial relief, was adopted in order to enable the states to escape payment of their obligations. Much had transpired between 1787 and 1794, and, as a result, the need for a federal judicial remedy against the states was not nearly as acute as it had seemed to many at an earlier time. In the interim, over two-thirds of the debts of the states had been assumed by the federal government, and the state governments, for the most part, were able and willing to meet their remaining obligations. In 1790, when Secretary of the Treasury Alexander Hamilton proposed assumption, he estimated that the total state debt was about $25 million,[102] and he recommended that the federal government assume $21 million of this amount. Total state indebtedness was probably somewhat higher, perhaps $26 million, and the sum actually subscribed was less than that authorized, about $18 million; but, at most, remaining state debts amounted to approximately $8 million.[103] Moreover, during the 1790s and the ensuing decade, practically all of this indebtedness was discharged, partly out of state revenues and partly from federal credits, as wartime accounts between the states and the central government were settled.[104]

Had the financial condition of the states been as serious in 1794 as it was when the Constitution was adopted, the Eleventh Amendment might very well have failed to attract sufficient votes in Congress. In the absence of documentary evidence concerning the motives or purposes of those supporting the proposal, this, of course, must remain an object of conjecture. But Congress, at the time, was firmly controlled by Federalists who believed, as a matter of political doctrine and economic interest, that the satisfaction of public debts was a sacred obligation. If assumption had failed and the state governments had been pursuing, at the time, a policy of default and repudiation, it seems unlikely that the amendment would have enjoyed such widespread support. In any case, there is practically no evidence that Congress proposed and the legislatures ratified the Eleventh Amendment to permit the states to escape payment of existing obligations.

Even the cases in which states were sued do not project a picture of general fiscal irresponsibility on the part of the defendants, although there were certain kinds of claims—not actually debts—for which the states did not wish to be made answerable. None of the suits, it may be noted, was on public securities, paper, or loan certificates issued by a state. In *Vanstophorst* v. *Maryland* the debt was freely acknowledged and expeditiously paid. So, too, was the debt acknowledged by the state in *Cutting* v. *South Carolina,* but payment was withheld because of uncertainty as to whom the debt was due. Even Chisholm's claim was settled by the state, although the Eleventh Amendment already had been proposed by Congress. And New York's resistance to the Oswald claim does not seem to have manifested bad faith: the state was simply unable to verify the existence of a legal obligation.

The remaining cases in which states were impleaded—*Grayson, Moultrie,* and *Vassall*—raised far-reaching problems concerning the public domain and the sequestration of Tory property. Judicial inquiry into state policies respecting the disposition of public lands promised to open a Pandora's box. And, in Congress, as well as in the state legislatures, there was strong opposition to recognition of any liability to reimburse British creditors or to make restitution for the seizure of Loyalist property. In fact, this was the transcendent political issue of 1794 and 1795, when the Eleventh Amendment was under active consideration, as provisions of the Jay Treaty clarifying the rights of Loyalists came under attack in Congress and throughout the country. [105]

If opposition to recognition of Loyalist claims and to judicial inquiry into state land grants accounts for some of the support which the Eleventh Amendment attracted, it cannot, however, account for all. The roster of those favoring the amendment includes the names of ardent nationalists, as well as states' rights men. The congressional roll calls reveal neither geographic nor partisan divisions. A majority of virtually every state delegation in the House voted in favor of the proposal, and only two negative votes were cast in the Senate; both Federalists and members of the nascent Republican opposition overwhelmingly supported it.

Support for the amendment by states' rights men was, of course, to be expected. The amendment was a way to repudiate *Chisholm.* And, in the eyes of states' rights advocates, *Chisholm* cried for repudiation, perhaps not so much because it subjected the states to federal judicial process as because the principal opinions in the case expounded Federalist constitutional philosophy and all but denied the sovereignty of the states.

It is more difficult to account for Federalist support of the amendment. Perhaps some high Federalists such as Fisher Ames and Theodore Sedgwick [106] espoused the affirmation of states' rights implicit in the amendment grudgingly as a prudent expedient to deprive the growing opposition of a potential political issue and to secure their own political fortunes, but this is only conjecture. Other considerations may have been important in persuading Federalists, as the defenders of nationalism, public credit, and the sanctity of property rights, to back the proposed amendment. As noted previously, Hamilton's financial program, especially the assumption by the central government of state debts incurred in support of the Revolutionary War, had already secured the claims of numerous creditors. Many, probably most, had claims against their own states, and the *Chisholm* doctrine did not afford them a remedy in the federal courts. With assumption, a major portion of state debts was made payable without need for litigation and without reference to the citizenship of individual claimants. Moreover, by 1794, most states were, in fact, discharging their remaining obligations.

Suit against a state in the Supreme Court afforded an uncertain remedy at best, since the judiciary, in spite of its efforts to do so, was unable to devise a satisfactory process for compelling a state to appear and, more important, to satisfy an adverse judgment. The paramount tendency in American constitutional practice, and in nationalist theory, was already away from a system in which organs of the central government acted directly upon the states and their governments. [107] Such a system, in which the two levels of government from time to time would be arrayed directly against each other, was cumbersome, as experience under the Articles of Confederation had repeatedly demonstrated; and in this respect the Wilson-Jay theory of federalism enunciated in *Chisholm* was a false start, an anachronism in the mainstream of nationalist thought and in the development of American constitutional doctrine, although a few important vestiges of direct impact by national organs upon the state governments were to survive the trend.

Even before the *Chisholm* decision, an alternative for asserting federal judicial supremacy was in the making. Vested property rights and contractual obligations could be afforded federal judicial protection against state infringements—a transcendent objective in the Federalist scheme of values—in suits between private parties. Thus, the possibility of outright collisions between the states and the federal judiciary would be considerably reduced. This course was charted by the federal circuit courts in a series of cases beginning in 1791,[108] and these cases, unlike those in which a state was impleaded as a defendant before the Supreme Court, excited little opposition *at the time,* although they posed some of

the same substantive issues (e.g., the validity of state sequestra-
tions of British debts and property).

The practicality of actions against private persons for recovery
of British claims and for challenging the validity of state sequestration laws was soon to be demonstrated in the Supreme Court. As
early as February 1794, the Court decided a case which, in effect,
upheld a judgment of a federal circuit court against an American
debtor and in favor of a British creditor, whose estate Georgia had
confiscated during the Revolution. [109] When Georgia, after having
been refused its request to intervene as defendant in the proceedings of the circuit court, brought an original bill in the Supreme
Court to enjoin payment of the money to which it laid claim
under its sequestration statute, a jury rendered a verdict against
the state. Two years later, the matter was more directly presented
in *Ware* v. *Hylton,* a suit between private parties, in which the
court held that the Virginia sequestration statute of 1777 was
inoperative to discharge private debts owed to British subjects. [110]
The basis for this decision was the superior authority of provisions
of the Treaty of Peace.

Within a few years, other cases initiated in the federal circuit
courts and in the state judiciaries reached the Supreme Court on
writs of error, and claims of federal judicial supremacy over the
very subject matter which had aroused so much resentment in the
state-defendant cases were successfully asserted. Thus, in *Fletcher*
v. *Peck,* the Court, out of contrivance or necessity, at long last
passed—and adversely—upon the validity of Georgia's attempt to
abrogate the second Yazoo land grants. [111] The first phase of the
Yazoo controversy had reached the Court in *Moultrie* v. *Georgia,* a
case dismissed upon the ratification of the Eleventh Amendment,
and the general legal issues in *Fletcher* bore some resemblance to
those agitated in *Grayson* v. *Virginia.* Still later, in *Fairfax's
Devisee* v. *Martin's Lessee,* the Court rendered an opinion emascu-
lating Virginia's statutes forfeiting to the state the lands of British
subjects and Loyalists. [112] Specifically, the Court sustained the

claims of the heir of a British owner over those of a Virginia citizen who claimed the disputed tract by virtue of a grant from the state, which had earlier declared forfeiture and laid claim to the property as public land. In its opinion, the Court indicated that Virginia's statutes would be violative of the Jay Treaty if construed to forfeit the lands in question. The broad legal question presented in *Fairfax,* it may be noted, was somewhat similar to that involved in *Vassall* v. *Massachusetts,* although the remedy sought was different.

It would be too much to assert that nationalists, when they voted for the Eleventh Amendment, foresaw these later developments. But in 1794, they could take considerable comfort in the knowledge that the security of public credit had been guaranteed, at least as to a major portion of existing obligations, by national assumption of state debts and by the Hamiltonian funding system generally. Moreover, they may have understood quite well that federal judicial protection against impairments of contracts, tender laws, and other state infringements of property rights was possible, whether or not the states could be impleaded as defendants in the Supreme Court in suits instituted by individuals. To the nationalists, the amendment's implicit concession to state sovereignty may have seemed more formal than substantial, as later decisions, during the Chief Justiceship of John Marshall, proved it to be.

4

Basic Doctrines

Shortly after President Adams' announcement in January 1798 that the Eleventh Amendment had been formally ratified, United States Attorney General Charles Lee, in the much-delayed case of *Hollingsworth* v. *Virginia,* submitted to the Court the question "whether the amendment did, or did not, supersede all suits depending, as well as prevent the institution of new suits, against anyone of the United States, by citizens of another state?"[1] William Rawle and Edward Tilghman argued in the negative, and the Attorney General took the contrary view.

The Rawle-Tilghman argument turned on two propositions. First, they contended that the amendment was invalid, because the resolution proposing it had not been submitted to the President for his signature in accordance with Article I, Section 7, of the Constitution. The fact that such a resolution required for passage a two-thirds vote—a vote sufficient to override a presidential veto—did not make its submission to him superfluous, because the President might raise objections, which could reduce the initial legislative majority in favor of the amendment. Their second argument concerned interpretation of the amendment. They maintained that the words "commenced or prosecuted"

should be construed as meaning "to be commenced or prosecuted."[2] Thus, the amendment would be given prospective application, and the Court's jurisdiction would be restricted in future
cases only. "The spirit of the Constitution is opposed to everything in the nature of an *ex post facto* law, or retrospective
regulation."[3] Where, as here, the words of an amendment were
obscure and ambiguous, the Court should avoid a construction
opposed to the general tenor of the Constitution.

Replying to the first of these arguments, Attorney General Lee
noted that the Eleventh Amendment had been submitted in the
same way as all previous amendments. "The case of amendments is
evidently a substantive act, unconnected with the ordinary business of legislation, and not within the policy, or terms, of the
policy investing the President with a qualified negative on the acts
and resolutions of Congress." And in response to the argument
that the amendment should be given prospective application only,
Lee argued:

> From the moment those who gave the power to sue a state, revoked
> and annulled it, the power ceased to be a part of the constitution;
> and if it does not exist there, it cannot in any degree be found, or
> exercised, elsewhere. The policy and rules, which, in relation to
> ordinary acts of legislation, declare that no *ex post facto* law shall be
> passed, do not apply to the formation, or amendment, of a consti-
> tution.[4]

On February 14, a unanimous Court decreed that "the amendment being constitutionally adopted, there could not be exercised
any jurisdiction, in any case, past or future, in which a state was
sued by the citizens of another state, or by citizens, or subjects, of
any foreign state." With a single exception, all pending cases in
which a state had been impleaded as a defendant were swept from
the docket.[5]

Following the decree in *Hollingsworth* v. *Virginia,* over a decade
passed before the Eleventh Amendment was again considered and
interpreted by the Supreme Court. It was inevitable, no doubt,
that the amendment, as one of the few concessions to state

sovereignty in the Constitution, would be invoked in support of general states' rights doctrines, asserted in first one state and then another as local and national policies came into conflict. In reacting to such expansive interpretations, the Supreme Court, speaking through Chief Justice Marshall, formulated the basic law of the amendment in three opinions sharply circumscribing its potential impact upon the scope of the federal judicial power.

The first of these cases was *United States* v. *Peters,* a chapter in a protracted and bitter controversy originating during the Revolutionary War and pitting the government of the United States against the state of Pennsylvania.[6] In 1778, Gideon Olmstead and others, who had been impressed as seamen on the British sloop *Active,* rose up and took control of the vessel. While on its way to an American port, the *Active* was captured by an armed brig belonging to the state of Pennsylvania; the vessel was later libelled as a prize of war in the Pennsylvania court of admiralty.

Over claims by Olmstead and his associates that the *Active* was their exclusive prize, the court awarded them only one-fourth part, with the residue to be divided between the state and a third party assisting in the capture. Olmstead appealed to the committee of appeals of the Continental Congress, which sustained his claim. The Pennsylvania court of admiralty declined to accept the committee's decision, however, and directed that funds from the sale of the ship be placed in the custody of the state treasurer.

In subsequent proceedings, the Continental Congress strongly admonished the state as to its responsibilities, but to no avail. Moreover, Olmstead was rebuffed by the state supreme court where he had renewed his claims. The state treasurer, David Rittenhouse, in whose custody the disputed funds had been placed, died in the meantime; and when the Pennsylvania legislature in 1801 directed the new treasurer to secure the funds from Rittenhouse's heirs, the latter refused to comply with the requisition because of the conflicting legal claims. At about the same time, Olmstead brought suit against the Rittenhouse heirs in a federal district court, and in 1803 Judge Richard Peters of that court affirmed Olmstead's title. The governor responded with a message to the legislature in which he strongly critized Judge Peters' action on the ground that the state had been given no notice or opportunity to be heard. And he complained that the suit violated the Eleventh Amendment because the state was the real, even if not the nominal, defendant in the action. In the ensuing uproar, the state legislature adopted an elaborate resolution reciting the history of the case, declaring the decisions of the committee of appeals and of Judge Peters void as usurpations, and directing the governor to protect the Rittenhouse heirs from federal judicial process. With reference to the proceedings before Judge Peters, the legislature declared

> that the rights of this commonwealth, as a claimant and as the party substantially interested in the said suit, though apparent on the face of the proceedings, were unfairly passed over and set aside; that the said David Rittenhouse was not and ought not to have been considered in the light of a mere stakeholder, but as the treasurer and agent of this commonwealth, and that the jurisdiction and decree of the said Richard Peters hereon were entertained and made in manifest opposition to, and violation of, the last amendment of the constitution of the United States, and ought not to be supported or obeyed.[7]

In face of the state's threats, including the distinct possibility that the governor would employ the militia to prevent execution of the judgment, Judge Peters permitted the matter to lapse "for prudential reasons," and no immediate action was taken to carry the judgment into effect.

Olmstead revived his claim in 1808 with a motion in the Supreme Court for a writ of mandamus commanding Judge Peters to order an attachment and other appropriate process against the Rittenhouse heirs in execution of the 1803 judgment. In 1809, Chief Justice Marshall delivered the Court's unanimous opinion directing Peters to execute his previous decree. "If the legislatures of the several states," said Marshall, "may, at will, annul the judgments of the courts of the United States, and destroy the rights acquired under those judgments, the constitution itself becomes a solemn mockery, and the nation is deprived of the means of enforcing its laws by the instrumentality of its own tribunals."[8] Ultimate authority for determining the extent of the federal judicial power was not, he maintained, lodged in the legislatures of the states, but in the Supreme Court of the United States.

After reviewing the proceedings in the case, the Chief Justice rejected Pennsylvania's contention that Olmstead's suit against the Rittenhouse heirs in the district court was, in effect, a suit against the state barred by the Eleventh Amendment:

> The right of a state to assert, as plaintiff, any interest it may have in a subject, which forms the matter of controversy between individuals, in one of the courts of the United States, is not affected by this amendment; nor can it be so construed as to oust the court of its jurisdiction, should such claim be suggested. The amendment simply provides, that no suit shall be commenced or prosecuted against a state. The state cannot be made a defendant to a suit brought by an individual; but it remains the duty of the courts of the United States to decide all cases brought before them by citizens of one state against citizens of a different state, where a state is not necessarily a defendant. In this case, the suit was not instituted against the state or its treasurer, but against the executrixes of David Rittenhouse, for the proceeds of a vessel condemned in the court of admiralty, which were admitted to be in their possession. If these proceeds had been the actual property of Pennsylvania, however wrongfully acquired, the disclosure of that fact would have presented a case on which it is unnecessary to give an opinion; but it certainly can never be alleged that a mere suggestion of title in a state to property, in possession of an individual, must arrest the proceedings of the court, and prevent their looking into the suggestion, and examining the validity of the title.[9]

An examination of the proceedings revealed, according to Marshall, that the claims of the state had been extinguished by the decree of the committee of appeals in favor of Olmstead. Moreover, the proceeds from sale of the vessel had been paid over to Rittenhouse and held by him in his own right and not in his official capacity as state treasurer. In light of these conclusions—that Pennsylvania had no valid claim of title to the disputed fund and that the fund was not in the possession of a state officer in his official capacity—the suit instituted by Olmstead for recovery was not a suit against the state within the meaning of the Eleventh Amendment.

With the announcement of the Court's decision, the governor of Pennsylvania deployed the state militia around the home of the Rittenhouse heirs to prevent service of process in execution of the 1803 judgment. The United States marshal, having been denied access, enlisted a posse, and, for a time, an armed clash between the two forces seemed imminent. The state relented, however, when President Madison indicated that he would use his powers to enforce the Court's judgment. Moreover, other states, whose moral support had been anticipated, sharply criticized Pennsylvania's attitude, and probably influenced the outcome.[10] The state's humiliation at the hands of the federal judiciary became complete when the commander of the state militia was tried and convicted in federal court for forcibly resisting the United States marshal. In this phase of the case, also, the Eleventh Amendment was pleaded as a defense but found inapplicable by Justice Bushrod Washington in circuit.[11]

United States v. *Peters* was an important episode in the intensifying struggle over federal judicial supremacy. The Court had successfully asserted, against the pretensions of a state, ultimate authority to determine the scope of the federal judicial power defined by the Constitution. Moreover, the Eleventh Amendment, which stated an exception to that power, had been construed narrowly. A state could not assert its own immunity in defense of an individual party merely because the state claimed a proprietary interest in the subject matter of the dispute or a concern as to its outcome. Had the state's argument prevailed, the federal judicial power would have been exposed to serious erosion in future cases.

Peters did not, however, permanently dispose of the broad constitutional issues presented there. These issues—the locus of sovereignty and the nature of the federal union—were constitutional restatements of fundamental political and economic questions over which whole sections of the nation became arrayed in opposition to each other and to national policies. As such, these constitutional issues would not, in the end, yield to definitive judicial settlement, although the courts attempted again and again to provide a solution during the half-century following the *Peters* decision. Viewed in retrospect, the federal judiciary succeeded in enunciating a doctrine legitimating the outcome of a subsequent resort to arms; but the courts, like the avowedly political branches, were unable to check the centrifugal forces at work in the Union.

Following *Peters,* the assault upon federal judicial supremacy was renewed in *Martin* v. *Hunter's Lessee,* the sequel to the *Fairfax* case.[12] But in *Martin,* Virginia's attack upon the jurisdiction of the Supreme Court was based upon the sweeping contention that Section 25 of the Judiciary Act of 1789, providing for review by the Supreme Court of state decisions in federal-question cases, was unconstitutional. Neither Judge Spencer Roane of the Virginia Court of Appeals nor Justice Joseph Story, who wrote the Supreme Court's opinion, cited or discussed the Eleventh Amendment. A short time later, however, the amendment was invoked again in defense of state sovereignty.

In *Cohens* v. *Virginia*, the defendants had been convicted by a Virginia court for selling lottery tickets in violation of a state statute prohibiting all lotteries except those approved by the state.[13] In the trial court, they set up as their principal defense an act of Congress authorizing the District of Columbia to establish a lottery. This legislation, together with the implementing ordinance, they argued, granted them the privilege of selling lottery tickets throughout the United States, but the state court rejected this contention. The defendants thereupon sued out, under Section 25 of the Judiciary Act, a writ of error to the Supreme Court of the United States, claiming that the state court had passed adversely upon a claim of right and exemption under the Constitution and laws of the United States. The Cohens, it may be noted, were citizens of Virginia.[14]

The state, still outraged by the *Martin* decision, reacted sharply to this new challenge. A committee of the House of Delegates reported, in response to a special message from the governor, "that there is no rightful power in the federal judiciary, to arraign the sovereignty of a commonwealth before any tribunal, but that which resides in the majesty of the people."[15] And the legislature resolved

> that the Supreme Court of the United States does not possess appellate jurisdiction in any case decided by a State court.
>
> That, even if this appellate jurisdiction did exist in cases decided in a State court, between individuals, a State cannot be made a party defendant to any suit before a federal tribunal, commenced with the view to obtain a judgment against such State, or to reverse one obtained by it in a State court, or to any process or proceeding instituted in a Federal Court to correct or reverse a judgment entered in a State court for a penalty or punishment prescribed for the commission of any offence. . . .[16]

It was evident that the government of Virginia had not receded from the position taken by its Court of Appeals in *Martin* v. *Hunter's Lessee*—that Section 25 of the Judiciary Act allowing writs of error from the Supreme Court to state tribunals was unconstitutional. The *Cohens* case, however, was different from *Martin* in two particulars. Here the state itself was a party to the record, and the case involved a penal law, a matter of internal police regulation. These differences provided the state with additional grounds for contesting the assertion of federal judicial power. At the February term, 1821, counsel for Virginia, acting under explicit legislative instructions to plead to the Court's jurisdiction and to refrain from arguing the merits, moved for dismissal of the writ of error. The jurisdictional issue was elaborately argued by Senator Philip Barbour and Alexander Smyth, for the state, and by David Ogden and William Pinkney, representing the Cohens.

Senator Barbour contended that the Court was without jurisdiction for three reasons.[17] (1) The case did not arise under the Constitution or laws of the United States but under a municipal regulation of the city of Washington. Thus, jurisdiction failed as to subject-matter. (2) If there were any jurisdiction in the Supreme Court, it had to be original under that provision of Article III stating that in cases "in which a State shall be a party, the Supreme Court shall have original jurisdiction." But here the jurisdiction asserted was concededly appellate, and hence violative of the Constitution. (3) The judicial power of the United States did not extend, in any form, to this case. State criminal prosecutions, Barbour argued, must originate in state courts. There can be no original jurisdiction in the federal courts to try such cases. And the fact that a state is a necessary party to such prosecutions precludes the exercise of any appellate jurisdiction by the Supreme Court, whose jurisdiction in cases involving a state must be original under Article III. Therefore, there is no federal jurisdiction at all over cases of this kind.

This conclusion, Barbour said, was supported by proper construction of Article III in relation to the Eleventh Amendment. "Without reference to the character of the case, whether as criminal or civil, the judicial power of the United States does not extend to it, on account of the character of one of the parties. . . . It is an axiom in politics, that a sovereign and independent state is not liable to the suit of any individual, nor amenable to any judicial power, without its own consent."[18] To the argument of the Cohens' counsel that the state's consent was given by the constitutional provision extending the federal judicial power to all federal-question cases, Barbour countered that there were exceptions. The judicial power extended only to cases and not to all questions arising under the Constitution and federal law. For a case there must be parties before the Court, and under the Eleventh Amendment a state might not be impleaded as a defendant at the suit of a noncitizen. The *Cohens* case, of course, did not fall within the language of the Eleventh Amendment because a state and one of its own citizens were the opposing parties. But the amendment was addressed to those clauses of Article III extending the federal judicial power to controversies between a state and citizens of another state or aliens. There was no need to circumscribe by amendment the federal judicial power with reference to suits between a state and its own citizens because the Constitution conferred no such power.

> The words of the 11th amendment apply to the case of a citizen of another state, or the citizen or subject of a foreign state; but the reason is that only to them that the privilege of being parties in a controversy with a state, had been extended in the text of the constitution. It was only from them, therefore, that it was necessary to take away that privilege; but, when from those to whom a privilege had been given, that privilege had been taken away, they surely then occupy the same ground with those to whom it had never been given.... If I am right in the idea, that since that amendment, no matter what the character of the question, this court could not take jurisdiction in favor of the citizen of another state, or subject of a foreign state, against a state as defendant, it is equally true, that without the aid of that amendment, it never could take jurisdiction in favor of a citizen against his own state.[19]

At the conclusion of Barbour's argument, the question remained whether prosecution of a writ of error against a state was a suit to which the state might plead immunity. Continuing the state's presentation, Alexander Smyth turned to that question:

> If this writ of error be considered to be a suit in law, this court has no jurisdiction; for it is prosecuted against a state; and, by the 11th amendment to the constitution, no suit in law can be prosecuted by foreigners or citizens of another state against one of the United States. The amendment prohibits such suits commenced or prosecuted against a state. This seems expressly to extend to this writ of error, which, although not a suit in law commenced against a state, is a suit in law prosecuted against a state. This amendment, denying to foreigners and citizens of other states the right to prosecute a suit against a state, and being silent as to citizens of the same state, affords a proof that the federal courts never had jurisdiction of a suit between a citizen and the state whereof he is a citizen.[20]

With this, the state's claim to immunity was perfected. The federal judicial power, extending to all cases in law and equity arising under the Constitution and federal law, was qualified by the character of the parties. A state, being sovereign, could not be impleaded as a defendant at the suit of an individual, regardless of the subject matter of the case. The Eleventh Amendment expressly withdrew the federal judicial power originally granted, or construed, to reach suits commenced or prosecuted against a state by foreigners and citizens of other states, and the original grant of power never extended to suits instituted or prosecuted against a state by its own citizens. Finally, a writ of error contesting a state court decision in favor of the state, was a suit against a state and, as such, was precluded by the state's immunity. Thus, the federal appellate process did not include the power to revise or reverse decisions of state tribunals in favor of a state where the adverse party is either a citizen or a noncitizen, even though a claim of federal right had been asserted.

In responding for the Cohens, David B. Ogden asserted at the outset that he would not argue the constitutionality of Section 25 of the Judiciary Act, a question which he regarded as definitively settled in *Martin* v. *Hunter's Lessee.* And he thought that there was no serious question as to the applicability of that section, for the state's argument alone demonstrated the existence of federal questions upon which the Court's jurisdiction depended.

To the argument that Virginia was immune from suit, Ogden replied:

> It is no objection to the exercise of the judicial powers of this court, that the defendant in error is one of the states of the Union. Its authority extends, in terms, to all cases arising under the constitution, laws, and treaties of the United States; and if there be any implied exceptions it is incumbent on the party setting up the exception to show it. In order to except the states, it is said that they are sovereign and independent societies and therefore not subject to the jurisdiction of any human tribunal. But we deny, that since the establishment of the national constitution, there is any such thing as a sovereign state, independent of the Union. . . .[21]

The Eleventh Amendment, Ogden argued, was addressed exclusively to those provisions of Article III extending the judicial power to controversies between a state and citizens of another state and aliens. With respect to the judicial power conferred by those provisions, the amendment declared an exception, which in no way diminished the judicial power reaching federal-question cases:

> The original clause giving jurisdiction on account of the character of the parties, as aliens, citizens of different states, etc., does not limit, but extends the judicial power to the Union. The amendment applies to that alone. It leaves a suit between a state and a citizen, arising under the constitution, laws, etc., where it found it; and the states are still liable to be sued by a citizen, where the jurisdiction arises in this manner, and not merely out of the character of the parties.[22]

Concluding the argument for the Cohens, William Pinkney maintained that the appellate power of the Supreme Court over certain decisions of state tribunals was sanctioned by the Judiciary Act of 1789, which represents a "cotemporaneous construction of the constitution of great weight."[23]   Such power, he asserted, is essential to maintenance of the Union, especially in criminal cases raising federal questions, where state pride and popular prejudices may be particularly strong. Finally, in answer to the claim that review by writ of error was a suit against the state, Pinkney reasoned that the process here was not a suit. A reversal of the judgment below would leave things as they were before the judgment. Moreover, a state was not compelled to appear in answer to the writ, and the Supreme Court, in reversing a state court judgment, acted directly upon the state tribunal and only incidentally upon the state.[24]

In March 1821, the motion to dismiss the writ of error was denied in a unanimous opinion by Chief Justice Marshall, described as "one of the chief bulwarks of American unity."[25] This description may be deserved, insofar as a judicial opinion may be a bulwark of national unity, for the supremacy of the Court as the arbiter of the federal system was vigorously asserted and defended.

Cohens v. *Virginia* provided Marshall, who had not participated in *Martin* v. *Hunter's Lessee,* with an opportunity to answer Virginia's sweeping claim that Section 25 of the Judiciary Act was unconstitutional.

As stated by the Chief Justice, the first and most important question to be decided was whether the jurisdiction of the Court was ousted by the character of the parties, one being a state and the other a citizen of that state. In answering this question, Marshall adopted the argument made by the Cohens' counsel: the judicial power of the United States extends to certain cases because of subject-matter and to others because of the character of the parties, but the one basis for asserting the power does not qualify or limit the other. While a sovereign state is not suable except by its own consent, "its consent is not requisite in each particular case."[26] It may be given by a general instrument, and such consent, according to the Chief Justice, was granted by the clauses of Article III extending the judicial power to federal-question cases and to controversies between the states and specified parties. Each basis for the assertion of the federal judicial power, moreover, is independent of the other.[27]

If the judicial power of the United States in federal-question cases extends to controversies between a state and its own citizens, it may follow, as Ogden and Pinkney had argued, that a citizen may sue his own state on a claim arising under the Constitution or federal law. Chief Justice Marshall, however, was unwilling at this point to accept that conclusion, although he later introduced general language in his opinion which appears to do so. Initially, he suggested, probably with some misgivings, that such suits could not be maintained because a claim asserted at the original suit of an individual against a state technically could not arise under the Constitution or federal law. Thus, if a state were to lay an unconstitutional duty on exports, a citizen who paid that duty would be in the same position as anyone else who paid money by mistake.[28] The law raises an *assumpsit* to return the money, but a state's refusal to comply may be no more a violation of the Constitution than a state's failure to comply with any other promise. Other illustrations are furnished by state statutes which, in violation of the Constitution or a federal treaty, purported to sequester debts or to escheat private property. In these cases, an action against the debtor or the occupant of the land would lie, because an invalid state statute could not extinguish any legal right or title. But no suit by the claimant against the state could be instituted in order to obtain indemnification or damages, for no such equivalent is secured by the Constitution or federal law.

Quite different, of course, were situations in which the individual refused to comply with an allegedly unconstitutional state statute, while asserting defensively a claim of federal right. Such cases arise under the Constitution or federal law in the sense that their outcome turns upon the existence of the asserted right. [29] These cases, of which *Cohens* v. *Virginia* was one, fall within the judicial power of the United States and the appellate jurisdiction of the Supreme Court.

There was the further question whether the Eleventh Amendment had diminished the judicial power in respect to cases arising under the Constitution and federal law. On this, the opposing counsel had reached contrary conclusions, and Marshall's answer was not free of ambiguity:

> It is part of our history, that, at the adoption of the constitution, all the states were greatly indebted; and the apprehension that these debts might be prosecuted in the federal courts, formed a very serious objection to that instrument. Suits were instituted; and the court maintained its jurisdiction. The alarm was general; and, to quiet the apprehensions that were so extensively entertained, this amendment was proposed in Congress, and adopted by the state legislatures. That its motive was not to maintain the sovereignty of a state from the degradation supposed to attend a compulsory appearance before the tribunal of the nation, may be inferred from the terms of the amendment. It does not comprehend controversies between two or more states, or between a state and a foreign state. ... Those who were inhibited from commencing a suit against a

state, or from prosecuting one which might be commenced before the adoption of the amendment, were persons who might probably be its creditors . . . .

The first impression made on the mind by this amendment, is, that it was intended for those cases, and for those only, in which some demand against a state is made by an individual in the courts of the Union. If we consider the causes to which it is to be traced, we are conducted to the same conclusion. A general interest might well be felt in leaving to a state the full power of consulting its convenience in the adjustment of its debts, or of other claims upon it; but no interest could be felt in so changing the relations between the whole and its parts, as to strip the government of the means of protecting, by the instrumentality of its courts, the constitution and laws from active violation.[30]

The implications of the Court's language are not altogether clear. Did the Chief Justice mean that the Court could, or could not, take cognizance of a demand by an individual against a state where that demand turned on a claim of right under the Constitution or federal law? While Marshall is not explicit, his language points toward a negative answer.

It is by no means clear why the Eleventh Amendment, by its terms applicable only to suits against states commenced or prosecuted by aliens or citizens of other states, should preclude suit by a citizen of the defendant state where the asserted claim arises under the Constitution or federal law. Marshall may well have realized this. He had already indicated, although not unequivocally, that a citizen could not institute a suit against his own state under the federal-question clause. The reason given was that such a suit technically would not arise under the Constitution or federal law. The Chief Justice may have read the Eleventh Amendment as simply precluding exercises of judicial power granted by the original Constitution over controversies between a state and noncitizens. If this was its scope and purpose, then the amendment would place the noncitizen in precisely the same position as the citizen, and the former would therefore be unable, under the federal-question clause, to institute a suit against a state. Marshall, however, slurred over this meaning, if, indeed, he intended to embrace it.

The problem is complicated further in Marshall's subsequent discussion. The Eleventh Amendment, he said, applies only to *suits commenced* or *prosecuted* against a state by citizens of other states or by aliens. A suit is defined as the "prosecution, or pursuit, of some claim, demand, or request."[31] To commence a suit is to demand something by institution of judicial process, and to prosecute a suit is to continue the demand. The objects of the amendment were to prohibit the initiation, in federal court, of suits against a state by certain parties and to preclude the continuation of such suits as had been previously instituted. But process by writ of error was not, Marshall maintained, a suit within the meaning of the amendment—at least where such process is invoked defensively to correct a judgment by an inferior tribunal. A writ of error acts upon the record and not upon the parties, and a state enjoys no immunity in such a proceeding.

Chief Justice Marshall seems to have entertained some misgivings with respect to this conclusion, however, as he shifted his grounds:

> But should we in this be mistaken, the error does not affect the case before the court. If this writ of error be a suit in the sense of the 11th amendment, it is not a suit commenced or prosecuted "by a citizen of another state, or by a citizen or subject of any foreign state." It is not, then, within the amendment, but is governed entirely by the constitution as originally framed, and we have already seen, that in its origin, the judicial power was extended to all cases arising under the constitution or laws of the United States, without respect to parties.[32]

This statement appears to run counter to the suggestion made previously in the Court's opinion that the original Constitution and the Eleventh Amendment should be read as precluding suits instituted by individuals against a state, even though based on a claim arising under the Constitution or federal law. Moreover, Marshall's dictum, if so interpreted, creates a curious constitutional paradox: a citizen with a claim under the Constitution or federal law against his own state might sue in the federal courts, while a citizen of another state or an alien, parties exercising much less, if any, influence upon the government of the state for its beneficence, would be denied a federal remedy. Sixty-nine years later, this suggestion was expressly disavowed.[33]

The jurisdictional holding in *Cohens* v. *Virginia* was strongly criticized, although an outright confrontation with the state was avoided when the Court, in a subsequent ruling on the merits, sustained the judgment of the state tribunal.[34] In Virginia, the legislature narrowly defeated a set of resolutions calling for constitutional amendments. Among these proposals was one stating "that the judicial power of the United States shall not be construed to extend to *any* case in which a state shall be a party, except in controversies between two or more States nor to any other controversies involving the rights of a State, and to which such a State shall claim to become a party."[35] The other proposals had even wider import for federal-state relations and would have undermined the Court's role as the arbiter of the federal system.

In Virginia, and elsewhere, influential voices were raised in opposition to Marshall's opinion. John Taylor, a leading spokesman for the extreme states' rights position, fulminated against the Court for embracing broad constructionism, which he regarded as destructive of state sovereignty and of the supremacy of the Constitution. The framers and ratifiers of that instrument, according to Taylor, did not intend to invest the federal judiciary with the power of adjusting and defining the respective political powers of the states and the general government.[36]

Spencer Roane, who objected also to Marshall's interpretation of the Eleventh Amendment, shared Taylor's view. The object of the amendment, he said, was not, as Marshall had argued, to relieve the states of the necessity of paying their debts at the suit of private parties. Rather, its purpose was to recognize the inherent sovereignty of the states and their immunity from compulsory appearances before the tribunals of another sovereign—the courts of the United States.[37]

Thomas Jefferson, too, thought that the Eleventh Amendment barred federal judicial review of cases in which a state and individuals were adverse parties.[38] And James Madison expressed reservations concerning the Court's reading of the amendment: "On the question relating to involuntary submissions of the States to the tribunal of the Supreme Court, the court seems not to have adverted to all of the expository language when the Constitution was adopted, nor to that of the Eleventh Amendment, which may as well import that it was declaratory as that it was restrictive of the meaning of the original text. It seems to be strange reasoning, also, that would imply that a state, in controversies with its own citizens, might have less sovereignty than in controversies with foreign individuals, by which the national relations might be affected."[39]   Madison, however, did not agree with the other critics that the Supreme Court had no appellate jurisdiction at all over cases decided by the state courts.

Evaluation of Marshall's interpretation of the Eleventh Amendment and of the countervailing arguments of his critics presents serious difficulties. As already noted, the debates in Congress and in the state legislatures were not reported, and consequently direct documentary evidence as to the intentions of those who proposed and ratified the amendment is meager. It is probable, however, that the amendment was addressed to the particular situation which called it forth, and it should be read in its historical context.

That there was no design, on the part of its framers, to effect a revolution in federal-state relations seems clear. Nor was the amendment intended by its framers to make explicit some dormant constitutional presumption that the states retained that complete sovereignty which immunizes them from exercises of the federal appellate process whenever an individual was an adverse party. In this respect, the amendment fell short of meeting the expansive claims regarding state sovereignty asserted by some critics of the *Chisholm* holding. The amendment, as noted earlier, was proposed by a Congress in which nationalist sentiment was strong, and even among the Federalist majority the proposal encountered only token opposition. Had the amendment been regarded as immunizing the states from the federal appellate process, it is almost inconceivable that it would have enlisted such broad support.

The text of the amendment indicates that its purpose was limited. It speaks of "any suits"—not of "cases" or "controversies." The latter, however, are the terms used in Article III to define the federal judicial power and the jurisdiction of the Supreme Court. In fact the word "suit" does not appear anywhere in the original Constitution. This term has a much narrower connotation than either "cases" or "controversies," particularly when read in conjunction with the additional phrase, "commenced" or "prosecuted." Its use in the amendment was probably calculated to delimit the federal judicial power solely with reference to proceedings like those in *Chisholm* and other cases in which a claim against a state was asserted by an individual. Moreover, until the argument in *Cohens* v. *Virginia,* seemingly it had not occurred to anyone to argue that the amendment deprived the Court of appellate jurisdiction over federal-question cases in which a state was a party, although at least three such cases had been decided by the Supreme Court.[40] In one of these, *Smith* v. *Maryland,* the jurisdiction of the Court was closely and ably contested without, however, so much as a suggestion by counsel that the state was immune from process on writ of error.

While the meaning attributed to the amendment by the Court's critics was too broad, that ascribed to it by counsel for the Cohens may have been too limited. The basic assumption in their argument and in the Court's opinion—that the judicial power of the United States extends to federal-question cases irrespective of the character of the parties and alternatively to cases involving certain parties regardless of the nature of the subject matter—is sound. There is no evidence at all that the one basis for asserting the federal judicial power was conceived, by those who framed and adopted the Constitution, as limiting or qualifying the other. And there is considerable evidence to the contrary. However, one may doubt the conclusion advanced by David Ogden that the Eleventh Amendment was designed to restrict only that part of the judicial power dependent upon the nature of the parties, specifically that derived from clauses extending the judicial power of the United States to controversies between a state and citizens of other states or aliens, without affecting, in any respect, the power over federal-question cases. It is obvious that the Eleventh Amendment was proposed and ratified to preclude assertions of federal judicial power in suits of the kind then pending. Although these suits had been instituted under those clauses of Article III extending the federal judicial power to controversies between a state and specified parties, at least some of them—*Moultrie, Vassall,* and *Grayson*—posed questions arising under the Constitution and treaties of the United States. It is unlikely that objections to impleading a state at the original suit of a citizen of another state or of a foreigner would have been any less vigorous if the basis for the asserted jurisdiction had been the existence of a federal question. That the amendment was proposed, and ratified, moreover, to preclude any original suit against a nonconsenting state by a citizen of another state or a foreigner, whatever the nature of the subject-matter, is indicated by proceedings in Congress. During debate on the amendment, the Senate defeated the Gallatin substitute, which would have permitted suit against a state where the asserted claim was based upon a treaty.

If the amendment was intended to preclude all suits against a state by citizens of other states and aliens—even where the asserted claim sounded in the Constitution or federal law—a doctrinal ambiguity results, and this appears to have infected the Court's opinion and to account, in part, for Marshall's ambivalence in disposing of some of the issues. The Eleventh Amendment, by its own terms, applies only to suits commenced or prosecuted against a state by citizens of other states or aliens. It does not, in any way, alter the remedies a citizen may have against his own state in federal court. If the judicial power granted by Article III reached federal-question cases irrespective of the nature of the parties, and if the amendment precluded suits against a state by noncitizens, even where the claim arose directly under the Constitution or federal law, then it may follow that the judicial power over federal-question cases still reached suits instituted by a citizen against his own state. This result seems anomalous, however, because the national interest subserved by permitting a citizen to sue his own state in federal court is certainly not superior, and is probably inferior, to that involved in suits by noncitizens, which the amendment barred.

It is possible that those who proposed and adopted the Eleventh Amendment simply did not think through this problem. But there is a problem only if the clause of Article III extending the judicial power to federal-question cases is interpreted as implying a waiver of state immunity to original suits by individuals who assert a claim under the Constitution or federal law. Marshall, it should be recalled, initially avoided the problem of a state's suability by suggesting that an original suit against a state technically could not arise under the Constitution or federal law. The suggestion, however, was not unequivocal, and it is placed in further doubt by his later dictum that, if process by writ of error is a suit within the meaning of the Eleventh Amendment, the amendment by its own terms would not bar a suit involving a state and its own citizens. The Constitution, as originally written, would be controlling.

The Chief Justice, however, was preoccupied with a problem concerning the extent of the Court's appellate powers over state court decisions. His dictum may not have suggested any retrenchment from his earlier conclusion that a state could not be subjected to an original suit by an individual under the federal-question clause. If Marshall did imply, as the Court later thought,[41] that the federal-question clause of the Constitution should be read as making a state amenable to suit by one of its citizens, he may have been very much mistaken. But evidence on this point is not conclusive either way.

A general waiver of preexisting immunity may, of course, be inferred from the provision extending the judicial power of the United States to "all cases arising under this Constitution, the laws of the United States, and treaties," but with somewhat less assurance than with respect to the waiver deduced from the more explicit clauses conferring federal judicial power over controversies between a state and citizens of other states, or aliens. Waiver may be derived, however, at least as plausibly from the federal-question clause as from the others, if the meaning of specific assignments of judicial power in Article III is determined in light of the framers' broad objectives: the preservation of national peace and harmony. The records of the Federal Convention contain no comment concerning the suability of the states under the federal-question clause, and there are only rare and inconclusive references to the matter in the literature on ratification.

The views of the First Congress are also inscrutable. Under the Judiciary Act of 1789, the inferior federal courts were invested with no explicit jurisdiction over controversies in which a state was a party.[42] Therefore, if the federal-question clause was construed as making a state suable by an individual, such suits could originate only in the Supreme Court of the United States or in the state courts.[43] As drafted in committee, the judiciary bill provided that the Supreme Court "shall have jurisdiction of all controversies of a civil nature, where any of the United States or a foreign state is a party."[44] The Senate, before passing the act, eliminated the words "or a foreign state" and inserted the phrase "except between a state and its citizens."[45] As finally enacted, the pertinent provision of Section 13 of the act stated that "the Supreme Court shall have exclusive jurisdiction of all controversies of a civil nature, where a state is a party, *except between a state and its citizens;* and except also between a state and citizens of other states, or aliens, in which latter case it shall have original but not exclusive jurisdiction."[46] But whether the inserted phrase "except between a state and its citizens" was intended to delimit, by statutory provision, a jurisdiction which otherwise might have extended to federal-question cases in which a state was impleaded, or was to declare and affirm an implicit constitutional limitation, cannot be determined.[47] In light of the later doctrine that the original jurisdiction of the Supreme Court flows directly from the Constitution and is not subject to congressional modification,[48] the second interpretation seems preferable.[49] However, no one can say whether this doctrine was anticipated at the time the statute was passed.[50]

In *Cohens* v. *Virginia,* Marshall may already have been groping for a distinction to enable the Court to recognize that the states were technically immune from suits instituted by individuals, without, however, yielding to propositions that would undermine the federal judiciary as the arbiter of the constitutional system. *Cohens* reaffirmed, in no uncertain terms, the power of the Court to review state court decisions turning upon federal questions, whether or not a state was a party. But there were lingering doubts that appellate review alone would afford adequate safeguards. Was an individual, citizen or not, to be completely barred from initiating a suit against a state which had infringed his federal rights?

Osborn v. *Bank of the United States* afforded Marshall a new opportunity to accommodate the principle of state immunity with the supremacy of federal law as interpreted by the Court.[51] In 1817 the Bank of the United States, without obtaining authorization from the state, established two branch offices in Ohio. Although banks chartered by the state were at this time subject to a tax on their dividends, the Bank of the United States was not taxed. The Ohio legislature delayed action on a measure subjecting the bank to taxation until 1819, a year of severe financial hardship. In February, only a few weeks before the opinion in *McCulloch* v. *Maryland,*[52] the legislature enacted a statute imposing an annual tax of $50,000 on each branch of the bank continuing to do business after September 1; other banks were made subject to a tax of $10,000 per year. The state auditor was directed to assess the taxes, and in event of nonpayment his agent was authorized to levy on the property of the bank and to seize notes and specie.[53]

When Ralph Osborn, the state auditor, was ready to levy the tax upon the Bank of the United States, he was notified that an application would be made to enjoin the proceedings. Later he received notice of a petition in chancery and a subpoena to appear in court. After being legally advised that the papers did not constitute an injunction, Osborn directed his agent, John L. Harper, to collect the tax. On September 17 Harper presented himself to the cashier of the Chilicothe branch and demanded payment. When the latter refused to pay the tax, Harper seized approximately $120,000 in notes and specie. He deposited $98,000 to the credit of the state treasurer and kept $2,000 as his fee. The remainder was restored to the bank a few days after the seizure.

On the day following the seizure, Osborn was served with an injunction directing him to desist from collecting the tax and from paying it out if collected. He refused, however, to comply with this order on the ground that the matter was no longer under his control. A few days later, a United States district court judge granted an injunction restraining the auditor, the treasurer, and the depository bank from making any disposition of the funds. And this was followed, in November 1819, by an injunction issued by Chief Justice Marshall restraining the auditor and the treasurer from disposing of the disputed funds. Early in 1820, the United States circuit court in Ohio heard argument on a motion for an attachment for contempt against Osborn and others who had disobeyed the injunction issued in September.[54] No decision was reached until 1821, when by agreement of the parties, a decree was entered directing the treasurer to restore the $98,000 and to pay interest on part of this sum. This order was made on the understanding that portions of the decree affecting interest, costs, and Harper's fee would be appealed to the Supreme Court.

The state treasurer, however, refused to return the money on the ground that no lawful warrant had been issued to him by the state auditor, who could act only in pursuance of an appropriation by the legislature. The treasurer was held in contempt and imprisoned. A writ of sequestration was issued against his property, and the $98,000 in his custody was seized, taken into court, and paid over to the Bank of the United States. An appeal was taken to the Supreme Court.

The case of *Osborn* v. *Bank of the United States* was decided in 1824, after having been argued twice before the Court.[55] In addition to posing some objections to proceedings in chancery, Osborn's attorneys raised important constitutional issues concerning the jurisdiction of the circuit courts in cases in which a state is substantially, but not nominally, a party, and the correctness of the holding in *McCulloch* v. *Maryland* that the Bank of the United States was a federal instrumentality and hence immune from state taxation. Henry Clay, the counsel for the bank, declined to argue the second question, but Chief Justice Marshall in his opinion for the Court presented an elaborate defense of the *McCulloch* decision.

According to Osborn, the bill was, in effect, against a state, and, because the bill vitally affected the state, it should have been made a party.[56] This would result in ousting the circuit court of its jurisdiction, for the Supreme Court was constitutionally vested, according to Osborn, with exclusive original jurisdiction over controversies in which a state is a party.

At a later point in the argument, the jurisdictional challenge was presented in a somewhat different form:

> The present suit is substantially a suit against the state. The 11th amendment to the constitution was intended to protect the state effectually from the suit of an individual, not to permit its sovereign

> rights to be drawn in question, and its property to be taken indirect-
> ly by suing its officers. . . . The policy which exempts the states
> from being sued in the courts of the Union, is the same, whether the
> case arise under the constitution and laws of the United States, or
> whether the jurisdiction is founded on the character of the
> parties.[57]

In replying for the bank, Clay argued that Ohio had not been, and
need not be, made a party to the record, despite its obvious
interest in the outcome. The jurisdiction of a court, he said,
obtains in a case where an interested party is omitted if an
effectual decree can be made against the parties who are present:
"The constitution merely ordains that a state, in its sovereign
capacity, shall not be sued. It does not ordain that the citizen shall
not have justice done him, because a state may be collaterally
interested." This, he thought, was the settled law of *United States
v. Peters*. Here, however, the state's interest was more direct, and
Peters was distinguishable.[58] So Clay offered alternative arguments
in support of the circuit court's jurisdiction.

> But even if the state be a party, that circumstance would not oust
> the jurisdiction of the court, *in a case arising under the constitution
> and laws of the Union. There the nature of the controversy, and not
> the character of the parties, must determine the question of juris-
> diction.*[59]

Thus, the federal-question clause of Article III was interpreted to
make the states suable in the federal courts, with Congress having
the power to designate the tribunals in which such cases might
originate. This argument had troubled Marshall in *Cohens,* and
Clay was undoubtedly aware that the Court's response in that case
was equivocal. In light of this, he sought to show that Ohio, if
considered a party at all, was really the plaintiff and that the bank
was the defendant in this proceeding. The bank's action, an
application for an injunction, was substantially defensive in character.[60]

After reargument of the case, the Court rendered its decision in an opinion by Chief Justice Marshall. Justice Johnson dissented on the ground that neither the charter nor the Constitution authorized the bank to bring an action of this kind in federal court. Marshall, on the other hand, interpreted the charter as explicitly conferring upon the bank the right to sue in the federal courts. In his view, any suit instituted by the bank arose under federal law because the bank itself, together with its legal capacities, was a creature of a federal charter. And the fact that such suits may involve general questions of law does not withdraw them from the jurisdiction of federal tribunals.

The question remained whether the bank had pursued the proper remedy. As stated by Marshall, "the true inquiry is, whether an injunction can be issued to restrain a person, who is a state officer, from performing any official act enjoined by statute; and whether a court of equity can decree restitution, if the act be performed."[61] To answer this question, the Chief Justice assumed, for sake of analysis, that the state statute under which Osborn had acted was unconstitutional. The appellants had conceded that a void statute affords no protection to the person executing it. This was a vital admission, having far-reaching consequences for state immunity under the federal-question clause, and Marshall was quick to affirm it. The appellants, however, contended that the proper remedy was at law—a suit for trespass—rather than in equity; but the Court held otherwise on the ground that the action here was not a casual trespass. An injunction was the appropriate remedy to protect the bank from conduct threatening destruction of its franchise. In answer to Osborn's argument that the suit was improper because the real party, the state, was not impleaded, Marshall asserted that the real party's agent may be held accountable if the principal cannot be brought before the Court.

Osborn's most cogent challenge to the jurisdiction of the circuit court was based upon the claim that the suit was, in effect, against a state, and, hence, barred by the Constitution and by the

Eleventh Amendment. In responding, Marshall seems to have appreciated fully the differences between the state interests asserted in *Peters* and those in *Osborn*. Pennsylvania's interest in *Peters* had been indirect, but, as the Chief Justice conceded, Ohio's stake in *Osborn* was immediate. An agent of the state acting under the color of a state statute had been impleaded as a defendant in a federal court with respect to property taken into his custody in behalf of the state. But the direct interest of the state was not dispositive of the jurisdictional issue. Emphasizing that the Union might be disrupted if agents of a state could not be held accountable for their acts in federal court,[62] the Chief Justice concluded that the Eleventh Amendment applied only to cases in which the state was a party to the record:

> It may, we think, be laid down as a rule which admits of no exception, that, in all cases where jurisdiction depends on the party, it is the party named in the record. Consequently, the 11th amendment, which restrains the jurisdiction granted by the constitution over suits against states, is, of necessity, limited to those in which a state is a party on the record. The amendment has its full effect, if the constitution be construed as it would have been construed, had the jurisdiction of the court never been extended to suits brought against a state, by the citizens of another state, or by aliens.[63]

Thus, with respect to that branch of the federal judicial power extending to controversies involving certain parties, the absolute jurisdictional test approved in *Osborn* is whether those parties are named in the record. Conversely, since the Eleventh Amendment imposes a limitation upon the federal judicial power with reference to certain parties—the states—that limitation applies only in cases in which the state is impleaded by name.

In stating that the Eleventh Amendment applies only to suits in which a state is named as a formal party to the record, Marshall inadvertently left the impression that an individual with a claim against a state could circumvent the amendment simply by framing his action against an officer of the state, without naming the state itself as a defendant. This would have reduced the amendment to little more than a formalistic test. The Chief Justice, however, almost certainly did not intend to go that far, for immediately after enunciating the principle that the amendment applies only to cases in which the state is a nominal defendant, he added:

> The state not being a party on the record, and the court having jurisdiction over those who are parties on the record, the true question is, not one of jurisdiction, but whether, in the exercise of its jurisdiction, the court ought to make a decree against the defendants; *whether they are to be considered as having a real interest, or as being only nominal parties.*[64]

The foregoing paragraph makes clear that the Chief Justice, in advancing the nominal-party rule as one admitting of "no exception," was addressing himself to the issue of jurisdiction, narrowly conceived, and nothing more. The fact that the Eleventh Amendment does not oust the federal courts of jurisdiction over suits brought against state officers does not mean that in such a suit a decree against the officer upon the merits would necessarily follow, even if the statute under which he acted were adjudged to be void. The officer's interest must be real, or, to put the matter another way, he must be legally liable for some wrong. If such liability exists, justification in terms of official but constitutionally defective authority does not constitute a good defense. Upon these grounds the judgment against Osborn was, in most respects, sustained.[65]

When the doctrine of *Osborn* is stated in this way, the opinion of the Court four years later in *Governor of Georgia* v. *Madrazo* [66] appears to represent only a change of emphasis and phraseology rather than outright departure or retreat, which has sometimes been suggested.[67] Madrazo was a Spanish subject whose vessel, of Spanish registry, was captured by pirates. The vessel and its cargo of African slaves were condemned by a spurious court of admiralty not recognized by the United States. The slaves were purchased by William Bowen who, in an attempt to transport them into the Spanish province of West Florida, took them into Georgia, where they were seized by a United States customs officer. Acting in pursuance to acts of Congress and the state legislature, the customs officer delivered the slaves into the possession of an agent of the governor. Some were sold, and the proceeds were deposited in the state treasury, while the others were left in the agent's possession.

Madrazo filed a libel in a district court of the United States for restitution of the remaining slaves and the proceeds of the sale. The governor of Georgia was among those named as defendants, and the district court dismissed the libel. On appeal, the circuit court directed restitution, and this decree, in turn, was appealed to the Supreme Court.

Speaking through Chief Justice Marshall, the Court reversed the decision of the circuit court. In reaching this conclusion, Marshall noted that the asserted claim was for money actually in the general treasury of the state and for slaves in possession of the government. Moreover, there was no allegation that the state's possession of either the slaves or the money had been acquired in violation of any federal law.

> The claim upon the Governor, is as a governor; he is sued, not by his name, but by his title. The demand made upon him is not made personally, but officially.
>
> The decree is pronounced not against the person, but the officer, and appeared to have been pronounced against the successor of the original defendant, as the appealed bond was executed by a different governor from him who filed the information. In such a case, *where the chief magistrate of a State is sued, not by his name, but by his style of office, and the claim made upon him is entirely in his official character, we think that the State itself may be considered a party on the record. If the State is not a party, there is no party against whom a decree can be made.* No person in his natural capacity is brought before the court as defendant. This not being a proceeding against the thing, but against the person, a person capable of appearing as a defendant, against whom a decree can be pronounced, must be a party to the cause before a decree can be regularly pronounced.[68]

The test formulated in *Osborn,* to the effect that the Eleventh Amendment is inapplicable unless the state is the nominal defendant, obviously was recast in *Madrazo.* But, in substance, the *Osborn* doctrine was not repudiated. In that case the Court ruled that a state officer is suable for wrongs committed or threatened in pursuance of an invalid state statute and that the Eleventh Amendment, being applicable only to cases in which a state is formally impleaded as a defendant, interposed no bar to such proceedings. The *Madrazo* test concedes that the Eleventh Amendment is applicable where the officer is not personally accountable. In such a case, involving official acts, the nominal party cannot be the real party. The real party must be the state for which the officer acted; hence the amendment is applicable. The result, however, is the same: if a state officer is personally accountable, he may be sued, and, if not, no remedy against the state is available.

With the opinion in *Madrazo,* the basic judicial gloss on the Eleventh Amendment was complete, and most later cases were applications and elaborations of rules formulated by Chief Justice Marshall. With the singular exception of the *Madrazo* case, Marshall's decisions had rejected the claims asserted by or in behalf of the state under the Eleventh Amendment. *Peters* had established that the amendment did not bar a proceeding in whose outcome a state was consequentially but significantly interested. In *Cohens,* the Court had, in effect, denied the applicability of the amendment as a limitation upon its appellate jurisdiction over federal-question cases. Finally, the general doctrine of *Osborn* that a state officer may be sued in law or equity for wrongs done or threatened, even though his acts are defended upon the basis of official but constitutionally defective authorization, afforded a potential remedy that partly mooted the issue of a state's suability under the federal-question clause. As a consequence of these opinions, the constitutional impact of the Eleventh Amendment upon federal-state relations was sharply restricted.

5

Suits Against Officers

Despite its potential as a basis for establishing, at the instance of individual suitors, federal judicial control over state officers and, through them, over state action allegedly violative of their rights, the *Osborn* doctrine was permitted to lapse into virtual dormancy for nearly a half century. Few suits were instituted by individuals against state officers in the inferior federal courts until after the Civil War, so that, for a time, judicial construction of the Eleventh Amendment was almost suspended. However, in the last quarter of the nineteenth and the early years of the twentieth century, the amendment again became the object of much judicial attention. Pressures for direct and expeditious federal judicial remedies were produced by grievances arising, first, from postwar repudiation by some states of their bonded indebtedness and, second, from pioneering attempts by the states to regulate business enterprise. And, convergent with these grievances, although probably not intentionally responsive to them, were modifications by Congress of statutes conferring jurisdiction on the lower federal courts, so that those tribunals were made more readily accessible to individuals asserting that the action of state officers, consummated or threatened under the color of unconstitutional state legislation, deprived them of federally protected rights.[1]

Between 1873, the year of the Supreme Court's decision in *Davis* v. *Gray*,[2] and 1908, when it rendered its landmark opinion in *Ex parte Young*,[3] the Court decided about thirty cases turning, at least in part, on interpretation of the Eleventh Amendment. Of these, by far the greater number involved the applicability of the amendment to suits instituted against state officers. But the question whether in specific instances a suit against a state officer constituted a suit against the state was not the only problem, although it seems to have been the most persistent and elusive one arising under the Eleventh Amendment. Other aspects of that amendment received judicial attention, and its meaning, as earlier defined by the Marshall court, was clarified and, to some extent, modified. During this period the scope of the amendment was delineated in three important respects: (1) the principle that a state may waive its immunity and subject itself to suit in federal court was established; (2) the amendment was held to be inapplicable to suits instituted against political subdivisions of a state; and (3) the long mooted claim that a state may be sued in federal court by its own citizens under the federal-question clause was rejected, with the Court pointing to the adoption of the Eleventh Amendment as confirmation that the original delegations of judicial power under Article III were implicitly qualified by the principle of sovereign immunity.

The principle that a sovereign may consent to suit and thereby waive his immunity is an ancient axiom of Western jurisprudence, and this principle, during the early years of the republic, was expressed in various Court opinions.[4] However, in light of the language of the Eleventh Amendment explicitly restricting the judicial power of the United States, the question whether the power extended to suits instituted by a noncitizen against a consenting state posed some difficulty. The constitutional distribution of judicial power, both in theory and in practice, has been generally regarded by the Court as inalterable through consent or submission of the parties.[5] Nevertheless, the Court determined that the federal judicial power encompasses suits to which a state, though otherwise immune, consented. While the rationale for this conclusion was not fully worked out, it apparently rests upon the assumption that the Eleventh Amendment did not modify the delegations of judicial power to the federal courts under Article III, but rather that its purpose and effect was to restore to the states the immunity which was, from the first, implicit in certain of these delegations but erroneously denied to them in *Chisholm v. Georgia.*[6] Under this interpretation of the amendment, its language was subordinated to a doubtful reading of history, and the federal judicial power, as later understood by the Court to have been originally granted—subject to the immunity of the states—remains intact, with that power reaching suits instituted by the noncitizen against a consenting state.

The waiver doctrine, as developed by the Court, was subject to further elaboration in several opinions. The principle that the consent of a sovereign to suit may be qualified by the sovereign was applied to the states, and the Court conceded that consent could be limited to proceedings instituted in state tribunals.[7] In a few cases, the Court considered the means whereby consent might be granted, concluding that a state may waive its immunity either by statute or by voluntary general appearance in a proceeding already properly instituted.[8] Finally, the Court held that consent to suit, unequivocally given by statute, subsequently may be withdrawn without violating the contract clause of the Constitution, even though private parties had extended credit to the state in reliance upon the continued availability of a judicial remedy.[9]

During the late nineteenth century another aspect of the Eleventh Amendment was considered in *Lincoln County* v. *Luning,* a case in which a circuit court of the United States had given judgment against a Nevada county on its bonds and coupons in a proceeding instituted by a citizen of another state.[10] The county claimed that, as a political subdivision of the state, it was exempt under the amendment from suit in federal court. In unanimously rejecting this claim, the Court noted that its records for the past thirty years abounded with cases in which counties had been sued. And, as if this were not enough to warrant denial of the county's immunity, the Court added that "while the county is territorially a part of the state, yet politically it is also a corporation created by and with such powers as are given to it by the state. In this respect it is part of the state only in that remote sense in which any city, town, or other municipal corporation may be said to be a part of the state."[11]

Still more far-reaching was *Hans* v. *Louisiana,* in which the Court definitively rejected the view that the judicial power of the United States, under the federal-question clause of Article III, extends to suits instituted against a state by its own citizens.[12] It will be recalled that this view was advanced by counsel in *Cohens* v. *Virginia,* and that the Court's response, in an opinion by Chief Justice Marshall, was both ambivalent and ambiguous. The problem was long mooted, however, because, under the Judiciary Act of 1789 and subsequent amendatory legislation, the inferior federal courts were not invested with jurisdiction over federal-question cases as such, and these cases were left to the cognizance of state courts whose judgments could be reviewed in the Supreme Court on writ of error.[13] This situation changed in 1875 when Congress enacted legislation providing that "the circuit courts of the United States shall have original cognizance, concurrent with the courts of the several States, of all suits of a civil nature at common law or in equity, arising under the Constitution or laws of the United States, or treaties made or which shall be made, under their authority."[14]

Invoking this provision, Hans, a citizen of Louisiana, brought suit against the state in a federal circuit court to recover the amount of certain coupons on bonds issued by the state. In an opinion by Justice Bradley, the Court sustained the judgment of the circuit court, dismissing the suit on jurisdictional grounds. Conceding that the Eleventh Amendment was, by its terms, applicable only to suits instituted against a state by citizens of other states and aliens, the Court adopted the traditional view that the amendment was intended to correct the error of *Chisholm.*[15] Its ratification constituted confirmation by the people that the original delegations of judicial power under Article III were, in most particulars, implicitly circumscribed by the immunity of the sovereign from suit. Although Bradley's argument is "lawyer's history," the result he reached may very well have been correct, for there is practically no evidence that any of the framers of the Constitution even contemplated the possibility that a state could be sued in federal court by its own citizens under the federal-question clause.[16] Moreover, as a matter of sound constitutional policy, the decision in *Hans* v. *Louisiana* is defensible. If the decision had gone the other way, a curious anomaly would have resulted. Citizens of a state would have had a federal judicial remedy against the state which citizens of other states and aliens, because of the Eleventh Amendment, did not possess. However, in deciding the case as it did, the Court clearly did not preclude suits by citizens of a state against officers of that state where the citizens' claims arose under the Constitution, laws, and treaties of the United States. Hence, an important effect of the 1875 legislation was to afford the citizen with direct access to the federal courts in suits of this kind, where, formerly, only the noncitizen, invoking diversity jurisdiction, could proceed in those tribunals.

For the past century, the most persistent and perplexing issue arising under the Eleventh Amendment has been presented in suits brought against state officers and contested on the ground that such proceedings violated the state's sovereign immunity. At the same time, there were numerous cases in which suits against federal officers were resisted as actions against the United States and hence not maintainable without the government's consent. The two lines of cases pose distinct constitutional issues. Broad issues of federal-state relations are at least implicit in most federal court proceedings against state officers for acts done under color of office, and suits against federal officers sometimes pose, with peculiar force, considerations arising out of the separation of powers. Still, the Court has not differentiated between them, and precedents established in one line of cases have been freely invoked to legitimize decisions in the other, so that the two have intermingled and converged.

There can be scarcely a pretense that the results reached by the Court in cases involving the suability of public officers are wholly reconcilable.[17] Judicial debris has accumulated heavily in this area over the years as principles once pronounced to be controlling have been supplemented or displaced by others, often without the Court so much as distinguishing, to say nothing of overruling, earlier precedents. Between 1873 and 1908, judicial interpretation of the Eleventh Amendment, and of the immunity of the United States as well, in suits against officers appears to have passed through three discernible phases, with each leaving a legacy of precedents that are not wholly compatible.

The initial phase is best marked by the opinion of the Court in *Davis* v. *Gray,* the first of the post-Civil War cases in which a suit against state officers was challenged as one against the state itself and, for that reason, violative of the Eleventh Amendment.[18] In 1856, Texas conditionally granted to a railroad company extensive land tracts adjacent to its proposed right-of-way.[19] A new state constitution, adopted in 1869, declared that the lands previously reserved for the railroad and not already alienated by it were to revert to the state for benefit of the school fund. An ordinance enacted by the constitutional convention during the same year provided that settlers upon vacant lands previously reserved for the railroad, but now forfeited, could acquire parcels of such land from the state. After the governor and land commissioner, acting on the authority of this ordinance, issued land patents to certain settlers, the receiver of a railroad instituted a suit in equity in the circuit court against these officers to restrain them from "interference with or infringement of the land grant or land reservation of the said company."

In a rather loose opinion by Justice Swayne, the Court sustained the decree of the circuit court awarding the injunction on the substantive ground that the state's grant to the railroad company was a contract, which it could not constitutionally impair by subsequent legislation.[20] The argument that the suit was substantially against the state and, on that account, beyond the judicial power of the United States was brushed aside on the authority of *Osborn* v. *Bank of the United States.* According to the Court, that case decided three things:

> (1) A circuit court of the United States, in a proper case in equity, may enjoin a state officer from executing a state law in conflict with the Constitution or a statute of the United States, when such execution will violate the rights of the complainant.
>
> (2) Where the state is concerned, the state should be made a party, if it could be done. That it cannot be done is a sufficient reason for the omission to do it, and the court may proceed to decree against the officers of the state in all respects as if the state were a party to the record.
>
> (3) In deciding who are the parties to the suit the court will not look beyond the record. Making a state officer a party does not make the state a party, although her law may have prompted his action, and the state may stand behind him as the real party in interest. A state can be made a party only by shaping the bill expressly with that view, as where individuals or corporations are intended to be put in that relation to the case.[21]

The foregoing statement, delivered at a time when state sovereignty was in disrepute, is an extreme expression of the nominal-party rule—the rule that treated the Eleventh Amendment as a limitation upon the federal judicial power only in suits in which a state was named as a defendant on the record. To be sure, Chief Justice Marshall, when advancing the rule in *Osborn,* indicated that it admitted of no exception as a jurisdictional test. But as restated in *Davis* v. *Gray,* the test sanctioned a broader federal judicial power than even the Marshall court seems to have envisioned. For one thing, Justice Swayne conveniently ignored the gloss on *Osborn* that Marshall had provided in *Madrazo,* although the latter case had received the attention of opposing counsel. More important still, Swayne distorted a salient aspect of the *Osborn* doctrine when he intimated that a state's immunity under the Eleventh Amendment not only does not insulate its officers from suit for wrongdoings committed under unconstitutional state legislation, but also that the officers' legal liability may be enlarged to correspond to that of the state, precisely because the state cannot be sued. This appears to have been the essential thrust of his remark that "the court may proceed to decree against the officers of the state in all respects as if the state were a party to the record." *Osborn,* of course, did not support this unguarded statement, which might very well have been applied to make state officers charged with disbursement of public money liable for debts upon which the state had defaulted, because the latter could not be sued. Such an extravagant result was not reached in any subsequent case, but the decision in *Davis* suggests the great lengths to which the Court was then ready to go in subjecting a state, through its officers, to federal judicial control. That the Court sustained the circuit court order is astonishing, for, in substance and effect, the decree, granted at the instance of a private party having only an equitable interest in the lands, enjoined transfer of that property by its legal owner, the state, acting through its constitutional officers.[22]

For nearly a decade, the Court appears to have adhered, albeit with increased misgivings, to the nominal-party rule in cases in which public officers defended upon the ground that suits brought against them violated the immunity of the sovereign for whom they acted. While the rule was not used in the next case, *Board of Liquidation* v. *McComb,* the Court's decision there would almost surely have gone the other way if the case had come at a later time when a more sensitive, less formalistic, approach were in favor.[23] In *McComb* the Court encountered one variant of a problem that soon was to become familiar—the extent to which the federal courts were empowered to afford relief to the creditors of states that had defaulted upon or repudiated their indebtedness.[24] Most of these states were in the South and, as a consequence of wartime devastation of their economies, were hard pressed to liquidate an indebtedness incurred for internal improvements and other purposes. The temptation to repudiate was heightened by the fact that much of the public indebtedness was owed to out-of-state and foreign creditors. In all, about twelve states defaulted upon some of their obligations, but the policies of Virginia, Louisiana, and the Carolinas occasioned the most litigation by disappointed creditors.[25]

In 1874, Louisiana enacted a Funding Act designed to reduce its indebtedness by authorizing the state board of liquidation to issue a series of consolidated bonds to be reserved exclusively for current bondholders who were willing to exchange their old securities at the rate of sixty cents of the new issue for each dollar of the old. To these creditors some inducements were offered by the legislation: the state courts were specifically empowered to enforce the act, a special tax was to be levied without further legislative authorization, and revenues from this levy were earmarked for service and retirement of the consolidated debt. A constitutional amendment adopted by the people of the state shortly after passage of the Funding Act solemnly declared that the issue of consolidated bonds and the statutory provisions guaranteeing them constituted a contract, which the state could not impair.

Within months, however, the legislature approved a new act authorizing the issuance of some of the consolidated bonds to pay, at face, a debt owed to the Louisiana Levee Company. Under the Funding Act, the company was not eligible to receive any of the consolidated bonds. McComb, as well as other bondholders, in the meantime, had surrendered old securities in exchange for the consolidated issue. Alleging that the new act impaired the contractual obligation created under the Funding Act, McComb brought suit against the board of liquidation to enjoin it from using any of the consolidated bonds for payment of the debt due to the company and from issuing any other bonds in satisfaction of that debt. The circuit court granted the injunction, and the board appealed.

The board's challenge was based on two objections—that the proceeding was a suit against the state itself and that the action interfered with the official discretion vested in state officers. In response to the first objection, the Court, in a unanimous opinion by Justice Bradley, tersely noted that a state may not be sued. He answered the second objection as follows:

> But it has been well settled that, when a plain official duty, requiring no exercise of discretion, is to be performed, and performance is refused, any person who will sustain personal injury by such refusal may have a mandamus to compel its performance; and when such a duty is threatened to be violated by some positive official act, any person who will sustain personal injury thereby, for which adequate compensation cannot be had at law, may have an injunction to prevent it. . . . In either case, if the officer plead the authority of an unconstitutional law for the nonperformance or violation of his duty, it will not prevent the issuing of the writ.[26]

If the principle enunciated by the Court is unexceptionable, its application was at least doubtful. In sustaining the decree of the circuit court insofar as it restrained the board from using consolidated bonds to liquidate the debt owed to the company,[27] the Court reasoned that since the company had been induced to exchange at 60 percent of par value old-issue bonds on the security of the funding scheme as a whole, the act authorizing issuance of consolidated bonds to others constituted an impairment of the contract and, hence, was void.

While the result reached by the Court was not tantamount to a judgment for specific performance, it appears to rest upon the assumption, later repudiated, that a state officer who is not a party to a contract between the state and individuals somehow becomes personally liable on the contract in the sense that he may be enjoined from complying with a statute that impairs the contractual obligation. Thus, the liability of the officer, as *Davis* v. *Gray* suggested, was enlarged to compensate for the immunity of the sovereign for whom he acts.

The nominal-party rule made its last appearance as a controlling principle in the majority opinion in *United States* v. *Lee* (1882). [28] This was an ejectment action brought by a descendant and heir of Robert E. Lee against the United States and its officers, Frederick Kaufman and Richard Strong, to recover possession of an 1,100-acre tract known as the Arlington estate. The property had been bid in by the United States at a tax sale in 1864, and, for over a decade prior to commencement of the suit, was occupied by the United States as a national cemetery and military reservation. The plaintiff alleged that the tax title was invalid.[29]   In the course of the trial in the federal circuit court, an order was made, at the request of plaintiff, to dismiss the suit against the United States, the latter having formally declined to submit to the jurisdiction of the court. Proceedings against Kaufman and Strong were continued over objection by the Attorney General that the subject matter of the suit—property claimed and occupied for public purposes by the United States under color of title—was beyond the jurisdiction of the court. After the jury found for the plaintiff, the defendant officers, as well as the United States *eo nomine,* sued out writs of error.

United States v. *Lee* was not an easy case. It was argued twice before the Supreme Court, which ultimately divided, 5 to 4, in affirming the judgment of the circuit court. In his opinion for the majority, Justice Miller considered the jurisdictional objection of the United States as resting "on the principle that the United States cannot be lawfully sued without its consent in any case, and that no action can be maintained against any individual without such consent, where the judgment must depend on the right of the United States to property, held by such persons as officers or agents for the government."[30] This somewhat overstated the government's argument, but it was to this proposition that the Court opinion was addressed.

While Miller somewhat grudgingly conceded that a sovereign is immune from suit, he rejected the inference that officers of the sovereign enjoy such immunity even when the disputed subject matter is property held by them under title claimed by the United States. In answer to Justice Gray, whose dissenting opinion laid great emphasis upon English cases to the opposite effect, Miller replied that such precedents were not controlling for two reasons: the availability in England of the petition of right whereby the sovereign's claim to property could be judicially determined and the inherent differences between a republic and a monarchy, the latter commanding unique respect for property claimed by the sovereign.[31] A survey of American precedents, including decisions in the Supreme Court, Miller suggested, while establishing "the general proposition that in no court can the United States be sued directly by original process," yielded "abundant evidence that the doctrine, *if not absolutely limited to cases in which the United States are made defendants by name,* is not permitted to interfere with the judicial enforcement of the established right of plaintiffs when the United States is not a defendant or a necessary party to the suit."[32] This was a rather guarded reaffirmation of the nominal-party rule, and the "necessary party" qualification probably accounts for the majority's explicit disclaimer of the passage in *Davis* v. *Gray* to the effect that a court may decree against an officer "in all respects" as it would against the sovereign if the latter were not immune.

To the argument of Justice Gray that since the government could hold property only through its officers and that suit and recovery against officers not asserting any personal interest in the property were, in effect, against the government itself, Miller responded that the suit was an ordinary action against individuals to recover property. The individuals had defended their occupancy upon the basis of an invalid title, and such defense could not prevail. If it were to prevail, then the plaintiff would be deprived of his property without due process of law.[33] Judgment against the officers, moreover, did not preclude the United States from recovery by way of a bill to quiet title, an ejectment suit against the present plaintiff, or condemnation proceedings.

The decisions in *Davis, McComb,* and *Lee* represent the most extreme instances of judicial enforcement of a sovereign's legal obligations—at least with reference to disputes over property and fiscal matters—by affording remedies against public officers through whose agency the sovereign acted. Although these decisions have since been doubted, none has been overruled, and *United States* v. *Lee* was followed in cases involving actions against state officers occupying property claimed by the states.[34] However, the general principle underlying these cases, that sovereign immunity is assertable only when the sovereign is directly impleaded by name, was soon abandoned.

Within only months of the *Lee* decision, the question whether the judicial power of the United States over controversies involving certain parties is to be ascertained solely by reference to the nominal parties of record was answered in the negative. The occasion for this holding was presented by two original suits instituted in the Supreme Court by New Hampshire and New York, respectively, against the state of Louisiana and its officers.[35] Decided together, these suits were another chapter in the continuing struggle between Louisiana and her creditors, which had first reached the Court in *Board of Liquidation* v. *McComb.* Despite the Court's decision in that case, holding that the state's 1874 funding scheme was a contract (as the state itself had declared it to be) which the state could not impair, in 1879 Louisiana incorporated into its constitution a "Debt Ordinance" abrogating its obligations. Interest that had accumulated prior to

1880 was repudiated outright, the interest rate payable after that year was drastically decreased, the tax imposed to fund payment of interest and principal was reduced sharply, and tax revenues previously collected were diverted to general state purposes.

A large portion of the consolidated bonds issued under the Funding Act of 1874 was in the hands of eastern creditors. Since the Eleventh Amendment precluded suits against the state, these creditors sought other means of relief. Suits against state officers constituted one possibility. Another was that their own states might be induced to prosecute their claims under provisions of Article III extending the federal judicial power to controversies between states and investing the Supreme Court with original jurisdiction over such cases. Both New Hampshire and New York enacted enabling legislation, each permitting its own citizens having overdue and unpaid written obligations of other states to assign them to the state for prosecution. The assignor was required to bear all costs of the litigation, and he was entitled to any money that was recovered. When assignments were made to the two states, each asked for a decree holding that the consolidated bonds were a valid contract, that the defendants be enjoined from diverting tax revenues from payment of interest, and that the 1879 amendment be adjudged invalid.

The suits were, of course, calculated to circumvent the Eleventh Amendment, and they might have succeeded if the Court had adhered to the nominal-party rule that it had been applying in cases in which public officers were sued. The Court, however, decided that it must look beyond the record parties:

> No one can look at the pleadings and testimony in these cases, without being satisfied, beyond all doubt, that they were, in legal effect, commenced, and are now prosecuted, solely by the owners of the bonds and the coupons. . . . It is manifested in many ways that both the state and the Attorney General are only nominal actors in the proceedings. . . . While the suits are in the names of the States, they are under the actual control of individual citizens; and are prosecuted and carried on altogether by and for them.[36]

By looking into, if not beyond, the record, the Court accepted Louisiana's defense that this was only a "vicarious controversy" in which the plaintiff states had volunteered use of their names in order to overcome the obstacle raised by the Eleventh Amendment.[37] This, the Court concluded, could not be done.[38]

Louisiana ex rel. Elliott v. *Jumel* grew out of a more orthodox attempt by some of Louisiana's creditors to obtain judicial enforcement of provisions of the much litigated Funding Act.[39] Here state officers—the treasurer, auditor, and members of the board of liquidation—were made defendants in actions for mandamus and injunction to compel them to comply with the act, notwithstanding the state's abrogation of the legislation by the Debt Ordinance of 1879. Specifically, plaintiffs sought a decree directing the officers to use accumulated funds to pay the interest due on the consolidated bonds and to collect certain taxes to pay the interest and principal on these bonds. They also asked for an order enjoining the defendants from diverting tax revenues from payment of interest on the bonds. *Jumel* was heard on the same day that the New Hampshire and New York suits were pleaded, and the opinion of the Court was announced on the day that it rendered its opinion dismissing those suits.

The judgments of the federal circuit court denying both the mandamus and the injunction were sustained in an opinion by Chief Justice Waite. While conceding that the Funding Act had created contractual obligations that the state could not constitutionally impair and that the requested relief might have been afforded directly against the state if it were suable, the Court declined to grant such relief against officers of the state. The decrees sought by the bondholders were understood to require "the officers against whom the process is issued to act contrary to the positive orders of the supreme political power of the state, whose creatures they are, and to which they are ultimately responsible in law for what they do."[40] Courts, Waite said, may direct state officers to perform purely ministerial acts, but in these actions the plaintiffs were attempting to impose judicial control over the state in its political capacity. *McComb* was explained away as a situation in which the officers were trustees of bonds for which only certain creditors could apply, and *Osborn* was read as permitting injunctions against state officers with respect to the disposition of funds claimed by the state, only where such funds, in fact or in law, had not yet reached the state's treasury. In summary, Chief Justice Waite characterized the relief sought by the creditors as follows:

> The remedy sought, in order to be complete, would require the court to assume all the executive authority of the State, so far as it related to the enforcement of this law, and to supervise the conduct of all persons charged with any official duty in respect to the levy, collection and disbursement of the tax in question until the bonds, principal and interest, were paid in full, and that, too, in a proceeding to which the State, as a State, was not and could not be made a party. It needs no argument to show that the political power cannot thus be ousted of its jurisdiction and the judiciary set in its place.[41]

Justices Field and Harlan dissented in opinions developing a common theme. Since the Funding Act created a contract, which the state could not lawfully impair, subsequent acts by the state which worked such an impairment were utterly void. From this proposition, they reasoned that the duties of state officers toward the consolidated bondholders under the 1874 legislation remained in force and that those officers could be judicially compelled to perform those duties, which, in their view, were purely ministerial.

The opinions of the Court in *New Hampshire* v. *Louisiana* and *Louisiana* v. *Jumel* constitute a turning point in the application of the principle of sovereign immunity. Prior to *Jumel*, there was only a single case, *Madrazo*, in which the immunity of the sovereign was successfully pleaded in defense of the officer who was sued. While suits against the state by name remained within the prohibition of the Eleventh Amendment, the nominal-party rule, insofar as it imported that only such suits were barred by that instrument, was quietly laid to rest; the formal requiem was deferred to a later day.[42] Henceforth, the Court's inquiry would focus on whether the state was an indispensable party in suits against officers, whether, in the *Osborn* sense, the officer's interest was only nominal, and more generally, whether a suit against an officer was, in substance and effect, against the state itself. In a fundamental sense, of course, the latter inquiry is based upon a doubtful premise. It is arguable that any suit against a public officer for action taken in pursuance of law is a proceeding against the sovereign. The latter can act only through its officers, and allowance of relief against the agent, if not tantamount to relief against the principal, at least may deter the agent from compliance with the principal's directives. This objection, however, may proceed too much on the theory that the government is identifiable with the sovereign. For the Court, the essential quest was for criteria that would accommodate, even if not reconcile, sovereign immunity with the rule of law.

A comprehensive statement of such criteria was essayed for the first time in *Cunningham* v. *Macon Railroad,* decided during the following term.[43] The case arose out of Georgia's repudiation of an indebtedness incurred when the state endorsed two issues of railroad bonds that were subsequently sold to private investors. In return for this endorsement, a mortgage upon the railroad was executed to the state, and when the company defaulted upon interest payments, it was placed in receivership. Shortly thereafter, the receiver sold the railroad to the state, which offered to exchange state bonds for railroad bonds of the first issue. Holders of the second issue, of whom the plaintiff was one, were to receive nothing, with the state asserting that its endorsement of that series had violated the state constitution. The plaintiff brought an action against the governor, the treasurer, and the company for a decree setting aside the sale, foreclosing a mortgage in favor of holders of the second series of bonds, and other relief. The federal circuit court dismissed the proceeding upon the ground that since a decree would affect the state's property by impeaching its title, the bill was, to all intents and purposes, one against the state.

With Harlan and Field again dissenting strongly, the Court sustained the judgment of the circuit court.[44] In an opinion by Justice Miller, the majority noted that there had been frequent attempts to compel the states to pay their debts by suits against state officers. In such cases, the central issue was whether the state was an indispensable party; if so, the proceedings, whatever the form, were beyond the jurisdiction of the federal courts. Miller acknowledged, however, that the Court, in the interest of dispensing justice to creditors who otherwise would have no judicial remedy, had sometimes "gone a long way in holding the state not to be a necessary party, though some interest of hers may be more or less affected by the decision."[45]

From the decided cases, the following guidelines were deduced. (1) Where state property, or property in which the state is interested, comes before the court in the regular course of judicial administration, without being taken forcibly from the government's possession, the court will render a decree; moreover, if the state becomes the actor, by suing or intervening, the court will dispose of the state's claims. (2) Where an officer is sued in tort for injury to person or property, the jurisdiction of the court is not ousted because the officer asserts official authority in his own defense. To make out a defense, the officer must show authority that is legally sufficient. (3) If the law imposes upon an officer a well-defined duty in regard to a specific matter, not affecting the general powers of government, those having a distinct interest in the performance of that duty may obtain appropriate judicial relief.[46] According to the Court, each of the cases in which relief against officers had been granted fell within one of these classifications. *Lee,* for example, though an action in ejectment, reserved the right of the United States to further proceedings to establish its title and, for this reason, the suit there was essentially a tort action against the officers for trespass. *Davis,* which was now

explicitly doubted,[47] and *McComb* proved more difficult to rationalize, but both fell within the third group of cases. The
majority did not think that the suit here was maintainable under
principles applicable to any of the foregoing classes of cases. To be
effective, the requested relief would necessarily operate against the
state as such and not merely against its officers in their personal
capacities. The state was not only an indispensable party but the
"only proper defendant in the case."[48]

The Court applied the guidelines announced in *Cunningham* for
over a decade, although not all (or even a majority) of the justices
supported them completely. Until the advent of the railroad rate
cases, which marked a new departure in judicial application of the
immunity doctrine in suits against officers, the cases almost invari-
ably turned on claims asserted under the contract clause. The
results in these cases, as well as divisions within the Court, reflect
the vexations inherent in granting or denying relief under that
constitutional provision in face of the immunity guaranteed to the
states by the Eleventh Amendment.

As an attempt to accommodate that amendment with the
guarantee that no state "shall pass any law impairing the obligation of contracts," the *Cunningham* guidelines took a middle
ground between two more extreme alternatives. The Court might
have sanctioned outright subordination of the amendment to the
contract clause, a course fraught with juristic difficulties, or it
might have treated the amendment as paramount over the other
provision. That neither was done does not signify lack of support
for these alternatives within the Court.

On the one hand, there were Justices Field and Harlan. Both
dissented in *Cunningham,* as well as in *Jumel,* but in some later
cases, they joined in opinions expressing the prevailing view that
legal and equitable relief may be afforded against an officer who,
under color of an unconstitutional statute, commits or threatens a
personal wrong. But Field and Harlan were prepared to go well
beyond this, to grant relief against an officer, even in the absence

of an allegation of tort, where his conduct was pursuant to an unconstitutional statute. Had this view won the acceptance of the Court at this time, the Eleventh Amendment would have been subordinated to the contract clause, with the officer, as a kind of surrogate for the state, made accountable for the state's impairment or breach of its contractual obligations.

At the other extreme were a group of justices who, while joining in the Court's opinion in *Cunningham,* soon expressed an important reservation concerning the criteria announced there. Although they agreed in principle that the federal courts could grant relief against state officers for torts committed under the authority of allegedly unconstitutional legislation, they interposed the important qualification that an officer should not be judicially compelled to disobey the positive orders of the state or held accountable for official acts taken pursuant to state directives. [49] The exception nearly engulfs the principle, and, if the Court had approved it, the contract clause would have been subordinated to the Eleventh Amendment as, indeed, a minority of the Court on one occasion contended it should be.[50]

The *Cunningham* guidelines, as already noted, represented a more moderate approach, which sought to accommodate state immunity with the substantive constitutional prohibition imposed by the contract clause. The resulting balance was extremely precarious. In applying these guidelines, the Court treaded a narrow and often indistinct path between judgments granting against state officers such relief as was tantamount to directing specific performance of the state's contractual obligations, and judgments withholding relief against these officers for wrongs for which official but constitutionally defective justification was pleaded. Results, moreover, were by no means predictable, if for no other reason than because the guidelines were not completely distinct nor the analytical categories mutually exclusive. To put the matter another way, it was possible for a particular suit to have features to which more than one of the three criteria were applicable. In such situations, application of one guideline might very well yield a result opposite to that reached if another were invoked as controlling.

Two cases decided during the 1885 term of the Court illustrate the close balance struck by the Court. The first of these was *Poindexter* v. *Greenhow,* one of the *Virginia Coupon Cases.*[51] Here, a bare majority of the Court reversed a judgment of a Virginia trial court dismissing an action in detinue against a state officer for the recovery of personal property that he had seized. In 1871, the state, in compromising its indebtedness, had agreed to accept coupons from state bonds in payment of taxes.[52] This obligation was repudiated in 1882 by legislation requiring that all taxes be paid in lawful money of the United States. Relying upon the state's earlier promise, Poindexter, as well as others, tendered coupons, but state officers refused to accept them. Later the officers, treating the taxes as unpaid, levied upon and seized property belonging to the plaintiff. Poindexter and others brought actions to recover their property and for damages.

Justice Matthews, who delivered the Court's opinions in the *Virginia Coupon Cases,* began with the assumption that seizure of property, if not legally justified, is a tort. From there, he reasoned that a law that unconstitutionally impaired the state's contractual obligation to accept coupons for taxes is not legal justification. Even if the officer had been directed to seize the property, he would stand charged of his own proper wrong. Nor was a suit against an officer in these circumstances a suit against the state. The latter, unlike a government, can manifest its will only through constitutional acts. In relying upon an unconstitutional law, the officer is stripped of his official character, and his wrong is a personal wrong for which he is answerable.

Quite the opposite result was reached in *Hagood* v. *Southern,* decided only a few months later.[53] Here the plaintiffs were suing to compel officers of the state of South Carolina to redeem revenue bond scrip which the state had issued in settlement of an earlier obligation. At the time of issuance, the state agreed to levy a tax for redemption of the certificates, and state officers were directed to accept the scrip in payment of taxes. These obligations were almost immediately repudiated, however, by legislation repealing the special tax and forbidding tax collectors to accept the scrip. The Court, again speaking through Justice Matthews, reversed the judgment of the circuit court granting relief. While South Carolina's repudiation of the scrip constituted an impairment of its contractual obligations, affirmative relief against the officer would constitute, the Court held, relief against the state barred by the Eleventh Amendment.[54] As portrayed by Matthews, the remedy sought by the plaintiffs was an order for specific performance of the state's contract. In a proceeding of this kind, the officer has no personal interest in the subject matter. Hence, he is only a nominal party. A judgment against officers "commanding them to perform official functions on behalf of the state according to the dictates and decrees of the court is, if anything can be, a judicial proceeding against the state itself."[55]

In juxtaposition, *Poindexter* and *Hagood* place in focus the impasse resulting from the Court's attempt to reconcile the Eleventh Amendment with the contract clause. The state could not proceed in the only way a state could proceed—through its officers—to levy upon the property of those who tendered coupons but otherwise refused to pay taxes for which such coupons previously were receivable. But, at the same time, the holder of such coupons could not obtain affirmative relief against state officers despite the fact that the coupons were constitutionally binding obligations upon the state. Neither the state nor its creditors could take much comfort in this situation. The state was unable to repudiate its obligations, although avenues for harassment remained open to it. The creditor, meanwhile, found that the marketability of his coupons was badly undermined even though the holder who tendered coupons in payment of taxes could successfully resist seizure of his property for unpaid taxes.

Poindexter v. *Greenhow* and the other *Virginia Coupon Cases* did not constitute the last judicial word on Virginia's efforts to repudiate obligations undertaken in the Funding Act of 1871. The Virginia legislature was both persevering and resourceful in measures calculated to destroy these obligations and, at the same time, to circumvent decisions of the federal courts. And few, if any, other matters were to spawn as much litigation for the Supreme Court of the United States. Among the cases to reach the Court, and sometimes regarded as the leading Eleventh Amendment case of the late nineteenth century, was *Ex parte Ayers* (1887).[56] The petitioner was the attorney general of Virginia, who, together with other officers, had been enjoined by a federal circuit court from bringing any suit against persons who tendered coupons in payment of their taxes. A duty to institute such proceedings had been imposed upon the attorney general and other commonwealth attorneys by a statute enacted in 1887—legislation that was a transparent attempt to evade a key ruling of the Court in the *Virginia Coupon Cases*. Specifically, this statute required persons who tendered coupons in payment of taxes to pay the amount due in lawful money, which was refundable on proof that the coupons were not counterfeit and that the tender was good. Upon tender of coupons by taxpayers, commonwealth attorneys were directed to test the sufficiency of the tender and the genuineness of the coupons, with the burden of proof placed upon the taxpayer. The latter's ability to offer such proof was seriously restricted by provisions rendering expert testimony inadmissible and requiring production of the bonds from which coupons had been detached. It was practically impossible to comply with this last requirement in most situations because the common practice had been to detach the coupons as they became due, and to exchange them, usually at a drastic discount, for money or other securities.

Several aliens who had purchased coupons for resale instituted an action in federal circuit court to enjoin Attorney General Ayers and others from commencing any proceedings under the statute, and in *Cooper* v. *Marye,* an order to that effect was issued. Ayers violated the injunction and was found guilty of contempt, fined, and committed to the custody of a United States marshal until purged of the contempt. He sought to secure his release by petitioning the Supreme Court for a writ of habeas corpus.

In an opinion by Justice Matthews, the Court held that the injunction issued in *Cooper* v. *Marye* was void and, therefore, that the petitioner should be released from custody. The Court's decision might have gone off on the narrow ground that the complainants in the original suit were without standing to seek the requested relief, since they had not tendered coupons for payment of taxes, and held only for speculative purposes. The adverse effect of the legislation upon the marketability of coupons was not, as the Court previously ruled,[57] an actionable injury. Although Justice Matthews did not ignore this objection,[58] he developed the broader thesis that the suit was substantially against the state and therefore was barred by the Eleventh Amendment. The rule, which he derived from *Cunningham,* was stated as follows:

> The inference is that where it is manifest, upon the face of the record, that the defendants have no individual interest in the controversy, and that the relief sought against them is only in their official capacity as representatives of the State, which alone is to be affected by the judgment or decree, the question then arising, whether the suit is not substantially against the State is one of jurisdiction.[59]

The Court, with only Justice Harlan disagreeing, had little difficulty in deciding that *Cooper* v. *Marye* was, in effect, a suit against Virginia.[60] The act enjoined by the circuit court was the mere initiation of litigation in the name of the state against allegedly delinquent taxpayers. Such an action, Matthews asserted, would violate no legal or contractual rights of the taxpayers, to say nothing of the plaintiffs. While those who tendered coupons in payment of their taxes might defend upon the basis of that tender against any action brought against them for nonpayment, tender was not the equivalent of payment so that the taxpayer was forever free from suit by the state. The relief which the circuit court had granted was against the attorney general and other officers in their representative capacity. "The vital principle" in cases in which relief was properly granted, "is that the defendants, though professing to act as officers of the state, are threatening a violation of the person or property rights of the complainant, for which they are personally and individually liable."[61] *Cooper* v. *Marye* was not, Matthews concluded, within the rule. While a state may not impair or breach its contracts, no process may run against it for doing so. The immunity guaranteed by the Eleventh Amendment precluded actions for damages, for specific performance, and for injunctions compelling specific relief by forbidding breach of contract. Officers of the state, not being parties to a contract between a state and its creditors, are not personally liable for breach of that contract. The remedy for breach, whether actual or anticipated, is on the contract itself, and the remedy operates only between parties to the contract. Thus, suit against officers for breach of a state's contract can only be deemed a suit against the state itself.

While the Court's opinion in *Ayers* reaffirmed the principle that the Eleventh Amendment does not bar suits against state officers for personal wrongs committed by them with official but legally deficient authorization, it spelled out as well a correlative principle: the mere fact that an officer acted or proposed to act pursuant to an unconstitutional statute was not, in itself, an actionable injury. So a state's impairment of its contractual obligations, even though unconstitutional,[62] was not chargeable to the officer, yet the latter could not defend his own wrongs by setting up, as authority, unconstitutional legislation, including legislation whereby the state impaired its contractual obligations.

From almost any perspective, the principle and its corollary seem to have been firmly established by the time of the *Ayers* decision. At least as early as *Cunningham* they appear to have been endorsed by the Court, and in the *Virginia Coupon* and *Hagood* cases they were applied with dramatically contrasting results. The importance of *Ayers* lies in its reasoned rejection of the claim that an individual may resort directly to the federal courts for an order enjoining a state officer from invoking state judicial processes for enforcement of an allegedly unconstitutional statute or regulation. If *Ayers* means anything, it is that mere institution of proceedings by a state officer in state courts is not tortious, despite the unconstitutionality of the legislation for which enforcement is sought.

The principles announced in *Ayers* and in its immediate antecedents were vigorously reaffirmed as late as 1891 in *Pennoyer* v. *McConnaughy*.[63] This case was a vehicle for a new attempt by the Court to explain and reconcile the results in earlier cases in which the Eleventh Amendment was pleaded as a bar to suits against state officers. Its resemblance to *Davis* v. *Gray* was close. A citizen of California had brought suit to enjoin the members of the Board of Land Commissioners of Oregon from selling certain swamp lands to which he claimed title by purchase from the state under a law enacted in 1870. In 1887, the legislature adopted a statute canceling certificates of sale unless 20 percent of the purchase price had been paid to the state before 1879. Acting on this authority, the board canceled the plaintiff's sale certificate and offered the land for purchase by others.

The federal circuit court's decree in favor of the plaintiff was affirmed by the Supreme Court in a unanimous opinion by Justice Lamar. The Court might have rejected the defense contention that the suit was barred by the Eleventh Amendment simply upon the authority of *Davis* v. *Gray*. However, that now-tarnished precedent, although cited, was not regarded as controlling. Differentiating suits that are not maintainable under the amendment from those that are, the Court declared:

> The first class is where the suit is brought against the officers of the State, as representing the State's action and liability, thus making it, though not a party to the record, the real party against which the

> judgment will so operate as to compel it to specifically perform its
> contracts. . . . The other class is where the suit is brought against
> defendants who, claiming to act as officers of the State, and under
> the color of an unconstitutional statute, commit acts of wrong and
> injury to the rights and property of the plaintiff acquired under a
> contract with the State.[64]

If the Court had left the matter there, its opinion would have
no special significance, for this general doctrine had been applied
since *Cunningham.* But, in order to clarify the doctrine and to
explain the results reached in some of the earlier cases, the Court
proposed a specific test. Where the plaintiff seeks affirmative relief
against the officer, the suit is, in effect, against the state, but
where only preventive relief is sought, the suit is maintainable. [65]
There were, to be sure, expressions in some earlier cases—*Hagood* v.
Southern, for example—to this effect, but in *Pennoyer* the nature
of the relief sought surfaced as a constitutional test which, as it
turned out, survived the virtual demise of the general doctrine,
which it was supposed to implement.

The demise of the general doctrine upon which *Pennoyer,*
Ayers, and their antecedents were predicated was shortly to begin.
Most of the cases so far decided by the Court had involved claims
asserted under the contract clause of the Constitution, and for
cases of that kind the general doctrine retained some vitality. [66]
But it was denied general application. Judicial interpretation of
the Eleventh Amendment with respect to the suability of state
officers entered a new phase with the advent of the railroad rate
cases, beginning in 1894 with *Reagan* v. *Farmers Loan and
Trust*[67] and culminating fourteen years later in *Ex parte
Young.* [68] As pressures grew for direct access to the federal courts
to test the constitutionality of state legislation regulating private
enterprise,[69] the applicability of *Ayers* was first discounted and
later disavowed by the Court.

The rate cases presented issues of due process and equal protection under the Fourteenth Amendment. Since that amendment,
unlike the contract clause, postdated the Eleventh Amendment,

the Court might have treated it as having superseded the earlier instrument, if the two were in conflict. The Court at one time came close to espousing this view, but it never quite did so. [70] Still, the opinions in the railroad rate cases indicate that for certain purposes the Eleventh Amendment was subordinated to the Fourteenth Amendment as it had not been to the contract clause, at least since the nominal-party rule was abandoned.

Reagan v. *Farmers Loan and Trust* was a suit in equity filed in a federal circuit court by the trustee of a railway company against the attorney general of Texas and members of the state railroad commission. At issue was the constitutional validity of freight and passenger rates fixed by the commission. The court found that the rates were unreasonable and hence violative of the Fourteenth Amendment and enjoined the attorney general and the commission from beginning any proceedings to recover penalties for violations of the rate schedule. The commission was also enjoined from issuing a new schedule of rates since certain sections of the statute under which it was empowered to act were invalid. The defendants appealed to the Supreme Court.

In one salient respect, the circuit court's order was similar to that which the Court had held void in *Ex parte Ayers:* it restrained the principal law officer of a state from invoking state judicial processes to enforce an allegedly unconstitutional regulation. Despite this similarity, however, *Ayers* was not regarded as controlling. In a unanimous opinion by Justice Brewer, the Court upheld the circuit court's decree except its order prohibiting the commission from prescribing a new set of rates. [71] According to Justice Brewer, *Ayers* established that an injunction may not issue to compel specific performance of a state's contracts. However, the injunction challenged here was sustainable under the principle that a state officer may be sued in law or equity for wrongs committed under color of unconstitutional authority. The defect in this argument lay in the Court's failure to identify the actionable wrong that the defendants were threatening. Mere institution of state judicial proceedings to enforce an unconstitutional regulation was not, according to *Ayers,* a wrong for which relief should be afforded. Denial of federally protected rights by the state courts should not be presumed, as the Court had repeatedly asserted, and if and when such denial occurred a remedy was available by way of review in the Supreme Court of the United States.[72]

To the attorney general's contention that the state was the real party upon which the relief operated, Justice Brewer made a novel reply:

> So far from the state being the only real party in interest, and upon whom alone the judgment effectively operates, it has in a pecuniary sense no interest at all. Going back of all matters of form, the only parties pecuniarily affected are the shippers and the carriers, and the only direct pecuniary interest which the state can have arises when it abandons its governmental character, and, as an individual, employs the railroad to carry its property. There is a sense, doubtless, in which it may be said that the state is interested in the question, but only in a governmental sense. It is interested in the well-being of its citizens, in the just and equal enforcement of all its laws; but such governmental interest is not the pecuniary interest which causes it to bear the burden of an adverse judgment. Not a dollar will be taken from the treasury of the state, no pecuniary obligation of it will be enforced, none of its property affected by any decree which may be rendered.[73]

There was, to be sure, ample precedent for treating the pecuniary and proprietary interests of the state as exempt from direct judicial interference in actions brought against state officers, but such interests had not previously been regarded as the sine qua non for immunity. By differentiating between the governmental and pecuniary interests of the state, Brewer deflected attention from the real and potentially more embarrassing inquiry whether the suit was against the officer in his representative, governmental capacity. Earlier holdings indicated that it was, and hence the action should have been regarded as one against the state itself. The Brewer doctrine, if not a tour de force, represented an astonishing inversion of precedent, for determination that the state's interest is governmental rather than pecuniary is hardly equivalent to finding that the officer is charged with an individual wrong. And the new doctrine yielded a result altogether incompatible with *Ayers* and other cases in which the individual liability of the officer was a precondition for relief against him.

To the same effect was *Smyth* v. *Ames,* where the Court unanimously affirmed an order of the United States Circuit Court for Nebraska enjoining the state board of transportation from hearing or determining any complaint against various railroad companies for violations of a state law fixing railroad rates.[74] The claim that the suit was against the state, while asserted in the lower court, was not pressed in argument, and Justice Harlan, speaking for the Court, summarily disposed of the jurisdictional objection: "it is settled doctrine that a suit against individuals for the purpose of preventing them as officers of the state from enforcing an unconstitutional enactment to the injury of the rights of the plaintiff is not a suit against the state."[75] But Harlan and his brethren apparently had some afterthoughts, if not about the stated principle then at least concerning its application.

The year after the *Smyth* discussion, the trend begun in *Reagan* was temporarily arrested. The case was *Fitts* v. *McGhee,* an appeal from a circuit court order enjoining the attorney general of Alabama and other law officers from instituting proceedings to enforce an allegedly unconstitutional statute fixing tolls on a railway bridge and from prosecuting, under a general penal statute, agents of the railway company for charging unreasonable rates.[76] In a surprising about-face, the Supreme Court, in an opinion by Justice Harlan, unanimously reversed the lower court. While the Court's decision was based partially on the ground that the suit should have been dismissed by the circuit court for want of equity, the main reason was that the action, in effect, was against the state. Despite its holdings in *Reagan* and *Smyth,* the Court thought *Ex parte Ayers* to be controlling for two reasons. Harlan argued first that the proceeding was not against officers for trespasses or other torts that they had committed or threatened. Rather, the suit was to enjoin the state from enforcing a statute by restraining its officers, upon whom the state necessarily relied. As such, the proceeding was as much against the state as if it had been named a party of record. Second, Harlan argued that the action was not sustainable on the ground that the officers were charged with a special duty to enforce the challenged legislation. This fact, he thought, distinguished the case from both *Reagan* and *Smyth*. To sustain an injunction in such circumstances would invite individuals to test the constitutionality of any state enactment by instituting proceedings in federal court against officers generally charged with law enforcement. At this moment, the Court was not ready to go that far.

Fitts v. *McGhee* provided only brief respite for states seeking to enforce, through their own judicial processes, rate regulations which were challenged as violative of the Fourteenth Amendment. *Reagan* and *Smyth* proved to be very much alive when, in 1903, *Prout* v. *Starr* was decided.[77] This case originated as a suit brought in the United States Circuit Court for Nebraska. By agreement, the parties were to abide by the decree in *Smyth* v. *Ames,* and meanwhile the attorney general was enjoined from enforcing the Nebraska statute. Nevertheless, the attorney general, through apparent oversight, filed an action for penalties in the state supreme court, which he later agreed to dismiss when the injunction was called to his attention. His term of office expired, however, before this was done, and when the new attorney general, Prout, refused to move for dismissal, the plaintiffs filed a supplemental bill in the federal circuit court asking that the original injunction be extended to restrain Prout from prosecuting the action. The circuit court granted the requested relief, and, on appeal, the Supreme Court unanimously affirmed. The result reached by the Court appears to have been fully justified on the ground that the supplemental bill was necessary in order for the federal court to perfect its jurisdiction and to avoid a conflict with the state tribunal.[78] But, in disposing of the case, the Court made clear that the Eleventh Amendment should not be construed in a way that would defeat substantive constitutional limitations, particularly those imposed by the Fourteenth Amendment:

> The Constitution of the United States, with the several amendments thereof, must be regarded as one instrument, all of whose provisions are deemed of equal validity. It would, indeed, be most unfortunate if the immunity of the individual states, provided for in the Eleventh Amendment, were to be interpreted as nullifying those other provisions which confer power on Congress to regulate commerce among the several states, which forbid the states from entering into any treaty, alliance, or confederation, from passing any bill of attainder, *ex post facto* law, or law impairing the obligation of contracts, or, without the consent of Congress, from laying any duty of tonnage, entering into any agreement or compact with other states, or from engaging in war—all of which provisions existed before the adoption of the Eleventh Amendment, which still exist, and which would be nullified and made of no effect if the judicial power of the United States could not be invoked to protect citizens affected by the passage of state laws disregarding these constitutional limitations. *Much less can the Eleventh Amendment be successfully pleaded as an invincible barrier to judicial inquiry whether the salutary provisions of the Fourteenth Amendment have been disregarded by state enactment.*[79]

In the hope of precluding federal injunctions restraining the promulgation and enforcement of transportation rates, some states, acting on cues supplied by the Court in *Fitts* v. *McGhee,* modified their rate-making procedures. Boards and commissions set up during the previous decade as regulatory agencies were stripped of much of their authority or abolished completely, as the state legislatures reverted to the earlier practice of prescribing rates directly by statute. At the same time, they were careful not to impose on any officer or agency a special duty to enforce this legislation. Under these circumstances, it was thought, the lower federal courts would be powerless to grant equitable relief against

state officials at the instance of individuals challenging the legislation. In still another respect, the new rate laws seem to have been
designed to preclude judicial review. They often included sections
subjecting violators to enormous civil and criminal penalties. So
staggering, indeed, were the potential sanctions against both railroad companies and their agents that violations for the purpose of
testing the validity of the rates were, at best, extremely hazardous.

Minnesota was one of the states enacting statutes with these
features, and this legislation was challenged in a suit that culminat-
ed in the landmark decision of the Court in *Ex parte Young.* [80]
Edward T. Young, the petitioner and the attorney general of
Minnesota, was committed to the custody of a United States
marshal for disobeying a federal circuit court order. Stockholders
of the Northern Pacific Railway had instituted an action in that
court against the company and certain state officials to prevent
compliance with and enforcement of passenger and freight rates,
which they alleged to be confiscatory. The complainants sought an
order against Attorney General Young enjoining him from beginning any proceedings to enforce the challenged legislation. The
court rejected Young's Eleventh Amendment objection that suit
was against him solely in his official capacity as attorney general
and granted a preliminary injunction restraining him from instituting any proceeding to enforce the freight rate statute.[81] Nevertheless, Young immediately filed in state court an action for mandamus in the name of the state, directing the railroad to adopt the
challenged rates. He was cited for contempt and committed to
custody until such time as he might have the mandamus proceeding dismissed. To secure his release, Young petitioned the Supreme
Court for a writ of habeas corpus.

By the time *Ex parte Young* was argued, the Court was in the
not unusual position of having at hand two sets of precedents
supporting opposite results. *Ayers* and *Fitts,* while distinguishable
from the *Young* case in some particulars, pointed to the conclusion that the injunction granted by the circuit court was void and

that consequently Young should be discharged from custody. But the major thrust of two intervening cases, *Reagan* and *Smyth,* was clearly the other way. In an opinion by Justice Peckham, the Court acknowledged the difficulty of the question and showed some uncertainty as to its resolution. Justice Harlan, whose views had undergone a drastic change since his dissent in *Ayers,* was again in dissent, but now on the opposite side of the issue.[82]

In the opinion of the majority, the challenged legislation was unconstitutional on two separate counts. First, the penalties imposed by the statutes in question—fines and forfeitures of at least $2,500 on the carrier for each offense and imprisonment of the railroad's agents for as long as five years—were deemed so enormous that the railroads would be intimidated into submission. The effect of the penalty provisions was to preclude the companies from obtaining a hearing on the reasonableness of the rates, a matter subject to judicial inquiry and determination. Under Minnesota's rate legislation, the options available to the carriers, according to the Court, were to submit to the rate schedules, which would work a gradual confiscation of their property, or, at the risk of losing all their property through fines and forfeitures, to defy the law. While conceding that obedience to a law or possible punishment for its violation are choices normally faced by those to whom the law applies, the Court asserted that there was a difference of constitutional dimensions between acts whose validity depended upon a fact determinable only through investigation (presumably, judicial investigation) and ordinary criminal statutes requiring no such determination and falling within the acknowledged power of the legislature. Where, under these circumstances, the penalties are so severe that such investigation by way of a hearing is virtually precluded, the legislation is void on its face.[83] Second, the Court held that the rates prescribed by the state were invalid because, if enforced, they would result in confiscation of the carriers' property.

The Court still had to answer the objection that the injunction issued by the circuit court was void under the Eleventh Amendment because it restrained the attorney general solely in his official capacity. Putting aside the question whether the Fourteenth Amendment had delimited the scope of the Eleventh, Justice Peckham thought that the injunction was sustainable no matter what effect the later amendment may have had upon the extent of the federal judicial power.[84] *Ayers* was explained away as a suit to compel a state, through its officer, to perform its contracts, while *Reagan* and *Smyth* were cited as affording "ample justification for the assertion that individuals who, as officers of the state are clothed with some duty in regard to the enforcement of the laws of the state, and who threaten and are about to commence proceedings, either of a civil or criminal nature, to enforce against parties affected an unconstitutional act, violating the Federal Constitution, may be enjoined by a federal court of equity from such action."[85]

To counter the petitioner's contention that *Fitts* v. *McGhee* had qualified this principle, Justice Peckham advanced an ingenious argument. In that case, he said, the act under which indictments were threatened was not claimed to be unconstitutional, nor were offenses under that act necessarily connected with the allegedly invalid rate statute. Under the rate statute, penalties for levying excessive tolls were recoverable by those paying them, and no state officer had any connection with such recovery. In such circumstances, a suit against a state officer to enjoin criminal proceedings was simply a strategem to test the constitutionality of the rate statute. But here the situation was different. While Minnesota's rate statutes did not *specially* charge the attorney general with enforcement of that legislation, by common law and statute he was *generally* charged with enforcing state laws. This general charge was sufficient, the Court concluded, to make him subject to an order enjoining any proceedings to enforce an unconstitutional statute.[86]

The remaining objection of the attorney general—that the injunction was invalid because an adequate remedy at law was available—was also rejected. On this point, the Court again referred to the enormous penalties chanced by those who defied the law in order to challenge the rates. And it noted that if such a test were risked by a single violation of the rate statutes, the carrier would at least have to acquiesce in the rates until the case was finally decided.[87] Equity, on the other hand, afforded more efficacious relief if the statute were held unconstitutional, and, the Court might have added, fewer losses to the carrier if it were not so judged.

Concluding, the Court reverted once more to the principal issue—whether the judicial power of the United States, as circumscribed by the Eleventh Amendment, extends to a suit against a state officer for acts not constituting individual wrongs. In an attempt to minimize, if not conceal, the shift from earlier doctrine, Justice Peckham stated:

> And, again, it must be remembered that jurisdiction of this general character has, in fact, been exercised by federal courts from the time of Osborn v. Bank of the United States up to the present; the only difference in regard to the case of Osborn being that in this case the injury complained of is the threatened commencement of suits, civil or criminal, to enforce the act, instead of, as in the Osborn Case, an actual and direct trespass upon or interference with tangible property. A bill filed to prevent the commencement of suits to enforce an unconstitutional act, under the circumstances already mentioned, is no new invention, as we have already seen. The difference between an actual and direct interference with tangible property and the enjoining of state officers from enforcing an unconstitutional act, is not of a radical nature, and does not extend, in truth, the jurisdiction of the courts over the subject matter. In the case of the interference with property, the person enjoined is assuming to act in his capacity as an official of the state, and justification for his interference is claimed by reason of his position as a state official. Such official cannot so justify when acting under an unconstitutional enactment of the legislature. So, where a state official, instead of directly interfering with tangible property, is about to commence

> suits which have for their object the enforcement of an act which violates the Federal Constitution, to the great and irreparable injury of the complainants, he is seeking the same justification from the authority of the state as in other cases. . . .[88]

There is no disguising the fact that *Ex parte Young* completed a mutation of constitutional doctrine which had begun in *Reagan v. Farmers Loan and Trust.* Had the doctrine of *Ex parte Ayers* remained intact, access to the federal courts by those asserting federal rights would have been stringently limited. The claimant would have been entitled to assert federal rights as a defense in judicial proceedings instituted against him by the state, and, in appropriate circumstances, he would have been able to obtain removal of such proceedings to the inferior federal courts. But the individual would have been unable to initiate proceedings against a state officer in the federal courts except where that officer threatened nonjudicial action, which was constitutionally invalid and which, at the same time, gave rise to common-law liability. Moreover, adherence to a rule requiring a showing of common-law liability for federal relief against an officer probably would have made subsequent application of federal equitable remedies against threatened infringements of civil and personal liberty, as distinguished from vested property rights, much more difficult. *Ex parte Young,* by indulging the fiction that an officer who seeks judicial enforcement of an unconstitutional statute is stripped of official justification and commits a wrong, opened the door to much broader federal judicial control over state policies.

The doctrinal development wrought by *Young* reflected the sympathetic preoccupation of the federal judiciary with the substantive rights secured by the Fourteenth Amendment. Although the Court never quite sanctioned the theory that the Fourteenth Amendment superseded the Eleventh Amendment insofar as the two might conflict, it liberalized the principles governing suits against state officers in such a way that the substantive rights guaranteed by the Fourteenth Amendment were accorded much broader federal judicial protection than were those asserted under the contract clause. The Eleventh Amendment, as read by the Court in apposition with the contract clause, yielded one principle governing suits against state officers, and quite another when construed in relation to the Fourteenth Amendment.

The reason for this difference does not lie simply in judicial recognition of the general rule that when two legal instruments of equal authority conflict, the more recent enactment prevails. This may have been a factor, but, if so, it was only an incidental one. Far more basic considerations were at work in shaping the Court's response. For one thing, enforcement of the contract clause in suits instituted against officers was beset with serious juristic difficulties. Since rights and obligations under a contract are binding only upon parties to that contract, direct enforcement of a state's obligation by way of suit against a state officer, if not tantamount to making the officer liable upon the obligations of a contract to which he was not a party, could only mean that a state is amenable, through its officer, to compulsory judicial process for the enforcement of pecuniary and other claims against it. In the Court's view, such a result ran directly counter to the prohibition of the Eleventh Amendment, whose central purpose, according to common wisdom and tradition, was to protect the states from federal judicial compulsion with respect to payment of their debts. But, if enforcement of the contract clause in face of the prohibition of the Eleventh Amendment presented paradoxes in suits against officers, so too did application of the Fourteenth Amendment. Inasmuch as the limitations of the Fourteenth Amendment are upon state action only—at least according to traditional constitutional theory—judicial implementation of these guarantees in suits against state officers presents a doctrinal dilemma. If the act of the officer who is sued is the act of the state, the Eleventh Amendment interposes a jurisdictional bar, and if the officer's act is not that of the state—if it is, essentially, a private act—then the Fourteenth Amendment is inapplicable. This paradox, which also may arise with respect to the contract clause and other prohibitions upon the states,[89] can be resolved, but the Court has not done so. Indeed it has seldom acknowledged the problem.[90]

The doctrinal departure wrought in the railroad rate cases may be better understood as a jurisdictional adjustment expediting and expanding federal judicial protection of certain substantive rights, which recently had become ascendant in the Court's scheme of values.[91] The principle with which *Ex parte Young* is identified reflected not only judicial concern for property rights but also the broadened conception of property that had been forged by the bench and the bar during the age of enterprise. This conclusion, admittedly, is somewhat speculative, and no direct documentary evidence can be adduced to support it; but it is something more than mere conjecture.

Claims asserted under the contract clause in suits against state officers had evoked a judicial response concerning the applicability of the Eleventh Amendment that generally coincided with the rather limited idea of property with which that guarantee had long been brigaded. Traditionally, the contract clause had protected vested property rights—particularly rights of possession, use, and alienation associated with the relatively simple agrarian and commercial economies of the early nineteenth century when that provision was first interpreted by the Court. Attempts to impart a broader meaning to the prohibition, specifically to transform it into a guarantee of economic liberty, generally had been unsuccessful.[92] By the last quarter of the nineteenth century, the judicial gloss on the contract clause was firmly encrusted, qualifications restricting its scope and efficacy had proliferated, and, while still retaining importance, it clearly had passed its zenith as a constitutional limitation upon state power.[93] The vested rights that the contract clause was understood to guarantee were, in fact, afforded protection in most of the cases in which state officers were sued. The principle that an officer is answerable for his own individual wrongs despite justification by way of a law unconstitutionally impairing the state's contractual obligations offered substantial protection to rights that had vested. At the same time, moreover, the principle that a state cannot be judicially compelled, by process against its officers, to perform its contracts was consonant with judicial protection of vested rights in the sense that while a creditor or obligee of the state may have a vested right in a state's performance of a contract to which it is a party, he has no vested right to a judicial remedy to compel performance. The individual who has financial dealings with the state is always on notice that, in event of nonperformance by the state, its immunity interposes a bar to judicial relief.

The conception of property with which the Fourteenth Amendment soon came to be associated was broader than that lying behind the contract clause. To be sure, the clause prohibiting the states from depriving any person of "life, liberty, or property without due process of law" encompassed vested rights. But much more was included, as both liberty and property were increasingly identified with economic freedom and with entrepreneurial activity in a burgeoning industrial age.[94] If, as the Court once stated and often intimated, economic liberty is the rule and restraint the exception, it is little wonder that the Court in *Ex parte Young* sanctioned procedures that effectively tied the hands of a state in matters of business regulation until the constitutionality of the state's policies received federal judicial clearance. Nor is it surprising, in this light, that the Court in *Reagan* would minimize the interest of the state in business regulation as "only governmental" and hence insufficient to clothe its officers with the state's immunity.

The immediate impact of *Ex parte Young* scarcely can be overstated. With the general principle that a federal court may enjoin state officers from enforcing an unconstitutional statute now definitively sanctioned by the Court, suits against state officers multiplied rapidly. The subordinate federal courts showed little disposition to interpret the *Young* doctrine narrowly and to restrict their jurisdiction by distinguishing that case, upon its facts, from those brought before them. In some instances, there was at least one substantial ground for distinction. For example, an objectionable aspect of Minnesota's rate statutes was the enormous penalties prescribed for violations. The penalty provisions of this legislation were given significant attention in *Ex parte Young,* with the Court holding that they rendered the statute unconstitutional on its face *and* that they afforded a basis for equitable relief—the legal remedy, partly on their account, being deemed inadequate. Despite the absence of such penalty provisions in legislation challenged in other suits against state officers, the circuit courts maintained their jurisdiction and afforded equitable relief. To be sure, an averment of irreparable injury, as is generally required in equity, was necessary to sustain actions for injunctive relief, but this requirement did not call for a recitation of anything like the situation supposedly confronting the complainants in *Ex parte Young.*

The implications of *Young* and its progeny for relations between the nation and the states were far-reaching, and the antagonism engendered by suits against officers was intense, verging in one instance, it was said, upon open rebellion.[95] The outcry was reminiscent of that following the decision in *Chisholm* v. *Georgia.* Although *Young* sanctioned suits against officers to enjoin their resort to state courts for enforcement of unconstitutional legislation, the Court at the same time reaffirmed the rule that federal injunctions may not issue to stay state judicial proceedings already in progress.[96] Conflict between the federal and the state courts in the exercise of their respective jurisdictions theoretically was precluded by application of this rule. However, since it made the timing of actions the crucial factor, federal-state relations were severely strained as those challenging state legislation raced to the federal courts to file their complaints, and state officers seeking to enforce the legislation made way, with equal urgency, to state tribunals.[97]

Even before *Ex parte Young* was decided, there were attempts in Congress to restrict the powers of subordinate federal courts and to modify their procedures in suits against state officers. The *Young* decision, of course, gave further impetus to these efforts. Within a few months after this decision, the Court administered a mild palliative in *Prentis* v. *Atlantic Coast Railroad* where it formulated a comity doctrine that was the precursor of several judicially developed rules limiting the powers of the lower courts.[98] However, the *Prentis* doctrine did not quiet the outcry against the earlier decision, if, indeed, that was its purpose. Congress was deluged with measures designed to undo, in whole or in part, the effects of *Ex parte Young*. Most drastic were proposals to withdraw from the subordinate federal courts any jurisdiction over suits instituted to restrain state officers from enforcing state statutes. Other bills would have prohibited the granting of injunctions in such cases until after final hearings or would have stayed federal proceedings if the state brought suit in its own courts to enforce its legislation. Congress adopted none of these measures, however.[99]

Specific aspects of the judicial procedures sanctioned by *Ex parte Young* met with particularly severe criticism. Under statutes and rules in effect at that time, federal judges could issue restraining orders without notice to the defendants, and these orders could be continued indefinitely. Interlocutory injunctions could issue after notice upon affidavits. In neither case was an adversary hearing necessary. The discretion vested in judges of the lower federal courts was practically unfettered, and there was widespread belief that this discretion was being exercised unwisely. Particularly objectionable was the fact that this discretion—which could be exercised to prohibit the principal law officer of a state from resorting to state courts for enforcement of state statutes—resided in single judges.[100] As Senator Overman of North Carolina, speaking for the Judiciary Committee, remarked during debate:

> I saw in Moody's Magazine last week that there are 150 cases of this kind now where one federal judge has tied the hands of the state officers, the governor, and attorney-general. . . . My experience is that the State is sometimes delayed a solid year in collecting taxes until a compromise is forced. . . . Whenever one judge stands up in a State and enjoins the governor, and the attorney-general, the people resent it, and public sentiment is stirred, as it was in my State, when there was almost a rebellion. . . . let one little judge stand up against the whole State, and you find the people of the State rising up in rebellion.[101]

The Senator's comments pointed to problems with which Congress was ready to deal.

The legislation enacted in 1910 originated as a Senate rider to a bill creating the commerce court.[102] It was designed merely to remedy procedural defects and, as such, fell far short of what some critics of the federal courts would have liked. Many senators and representatives from southern states, where there was a long tradition of opposition to federal judicial authority, as well as from the West, would have gone much further, but even so, this rather mild reform was approved by an exceedingly thin margin in the Senate.[103] As adopted, the measure provided that no interlocutory injunction suspending or restraining the enforcement of any state statute by state officers upon grounds of the statute's unconstitutionality might issue except after a hearing by a specially convened three-judge court. There was a requirement for five days' notice to the governor and attorney general, as well as to any other defendants, before the hearing. The statute further provided that a temporary restraining order could be granted by an individual judge if he believed that the complainant would otherwise suffer irreparable loss or damage, but the order would automatically expire upon determination of the application for the interlocutory injunction. To provide additional safeguards against long delays, there was provision for expediting the hearings and for direct appeal to the Supreme Court from an order granting or denying interlocutory injunctions. In enacting this remedial legislation while rejecting sterner expedients, Congress implicitly acquiesced in the assertion of federal judicial authority which *Ex parte Young* had sanctioned.

The history of judicial construction of the Eleventh Amendment following *Young* was, on the whole, anticlimactic. There were, to be sure, a few significant doctrinal developments. In *Philadelphia County* v. *Stimson,* [104] a suit against a federal officer, the principle enunciated in *Ex parte Young* was extended to permit proceedings to enjoin officers from acting in excess of their delegated authority to the injury of complainants, but the Court subsequently refused to go beyond this point. [105] The applicability of the Eleventh Amendment to suits in admiralty against a state was affirmatively determined, [106] and the question whether the governor of a state may be enjoined in the performance of executive and military functions was positively answered. [107] But otherwise the Court's decisions broke little new ground, if, indeed, these decisions can be regarded as having done so.

Of greater significance is what the Court did not do. The potential of *Ex parte Young* simply was not permitted to materialize. That decision ultimately rests on the fiction that an officer who proceeds under an unconstitutional statute or, as later extended in *Stimson,* in excess of power is stripped of his official authority, and, hence, a suit against him is not against the state. Had this fiction been pressed to its logical conclusion, it may well be that sovereign immunity would have been practically reduced to an exemption from suit *eo nomine.* But it was not so pressed. While the Court applied *Ex parte Young* with reasonable consistency in most subsequent cases, the immunity doctrine was preserved by episodic inquiries into whether, in substance and effect, a suit against an officer is against the state and consequently barred by the sovereign exemption.

6

Sovereign
Immunity and the
Rule of Law

Theories supporting the doctrine of sovereign immunity thus far have escaped attention, not because they are intrinsically unimportant but because their importance has not loomed large in the opinions of the Court. In fact, it is a misnomer to characterize the various rationales supplied by the Court as "theories" at all, for they fall far short of explaining the principles and rules which, in practice, delineate the doctrine and qualify its application.

Judicial defense of sovereign immunity has been, at best, episodic and equivocal. By and large, the judiciary has taken the abstract doctrine for granted, noting from time to time its antiquity and perdurability in Anglo-American jurisprudence. However, since the longevity of legal doctrine, especially in the area of public law, is not an altogether convincing reason for its existence and continuing authority, further justification has been ventured in some cases. Historical, political, and conceptual rationalizations have been advanced by members of the Court at one time or another, but even if taken together, they do not add up to a persuasive defense of the doctrine.

The historical rationale for the immunity doctrine was the first to appear in American judicial opinions. In *Chisholm* v. *Georgia*,

150

for example, Justice Iredell argued that English common law was in force in the states so far as it was applicable to their circumstances and unaffected by legislation.[1] Since the doctrine of sovereign immunity was already rooted in common law, his argument went, it was a part of the law of each state unless modified or revoked by statute. Iredell's conclusion that sovereign immunity was accepted in the colonies and in post-Revolutionary America is probably correct, but as we have seen, the English doctrine, by his day, had been reduced to largely a formal conception, through waiver on petition of right and by conferring upon certain courts jurisdiction over various kinds of actions against the sovereign. Moreover, Justice Iredell, like later critics of the *Chisholm* decision, did not accord sufficient weight to the fact that a waiver of the states' immunity was altogether consonant with and even, as then understood, necessary to fulfill the great purposes of those who framed the Constitution.

In the broadest sense, however, the rationale supplied by Justice Iredell is not unassailable. Although the English common law was to a large extent assimilated into the law of the states, the process was selective, and there is room for argument that the *public law* doctrines embraced by the common law—of which sovereign immunity was one—were transplanted only insofar as they were compatible with the political principles and governmental institutions that took shape and evolved during the post-Revolutionary and Constitutional periods. At least it would seem that the reception into the American legal system of common-law doctrines that are incompatible with those principles and institutions should not be inferred as a matter of course. If this view is correct, there is reason for doubting that sovereign immunity should have been recognized as a viable part of the common-law heritage in America, at least after the adoption of the federal Constitution. In fact some justices have occasionally voiced doubts, but on the whole, the problem has not been seriously analyzed.[2]

Sovereign immunity in English law was premised upon the nature of kingship. As the fountain of law and justice, the ruler, though under the law, was not subject, without his consent, to the processes of courts that were his creatures and instruments. This feudal theory of kingship, in which the immunity doctrine was rooted, survived the transformation of the royal office into nominal headship of the state. Even though sovereign power was depersonalized and eventually made democratically accountable to the English political community, the theory of power supporting sovereign immunity remained intact.

This theory of kingship has no validity for constitutional republics. Sovereignty, to be sure, is a viable, if somewhat cumbersome, concept for such regimes, and the proposition that the sovereignty of the king can be displaced by the sovereignty of the people—as it was through the American Revolution—may be conceded. Moreover, it is clear that both the sovereignty of the king and the sovereignty of the people presuppose the existence of ultimate power somewhere within political society. But the ramifications of popular sovereignty may be very different from those of kingly supremacy, not only for the institutionalization of political power but also for the relationship between the state and the individual. Popular sovereignty "suggests the idea of equals and equality,"[3] an idea not especially hospitable to exempting a group from legally enforceable responsibility toward its individual members.

Even so, in systems in which the will of the sovereign people manifests itself in the actions of their representatives—where popular sovereignty is largely identified with the will of the legislature as the constituent power—exempting state and government from judicially enforceable responsibility may be defended in principle. However, inasmuch as the will of the people is not identified with the supremacy of the political organs of government in the American constitutional system, the theoretical tension between popular sovereignty and the exemption of the state and government from suit is exacerbated. Since an early time, the Constitution has been regarded as the expression of the sovereign will, and the judiciary, rather than the legislative or executive branches, has been the preeminent expositor of the supreme law and, hence, of the popular will. In such a system, the rule of law, for better or worse, tends to equate with judicial review, and exempting the state and government from judicial redress where legal liability exists is a denial of the rule of law and presents an anomaly in the constitutional order. Nevertheless, the historical rationale for American acceptance of the immunity doctrine is the most persuasive of any offered by the Court.

A public policy rationale for the doctrine has also been voiced in some judicial opinions, but here too sustained analysis has been lacking, so that judicial expressions are scarcely more than hortative appeals to expediency. Justice Davis' remark a century ago that without the protection afforded by sovereign immunity, "the government would be unable to perform the various duties for which it was created,"[4] and Chief Justice Vinson's comment that "the government as representative of the community as a whole cannot be stopped in its tracks"[5] are fairly typical of judicial statements on the subject. Elsewhere, the immunity doctrine is treated as a necessary safeguard against judicial interference in the exercise of administrative discretion and in the fiscal and proprietary affairs of government.

A basic objection to this rationale, of course, is that the immunity doctrine, when applied, frustrates the performance of one of the most essential government functions, the dispensation of justice according to law, and, paradoxically, the doctrine is most commonly invoked to prevent or excuse judges from determining, on their merits, issues most peculiarly within their special competence. Still another objection to the public policy rationale is that, as a matter of experience, the dangers claimed to be inherent in rejecting sovereign immunity have rarely, if ever, materialized. There is simply no evidence that governmental operations have been embarrassed as governmental immunity has been constricted and liability enlarged through legislative enactments and judicial decisions. But even if the foregoing objections are overlooked, the public policy rationale is intrinsically very weak. No intelligible criteria have been offered by the Court for determining whether recognition of immunity is necessary to protect the government in the performance of its functions. To be sure, there are general rules that appear to relate to some apprehended need to insulate the government from certain kinds of judicial control over numerous activities and from virtually any judicial control over a few activities, but, at best, these rules express no more than outcomes of judicial choices that are probably more intuitive than reasoned. Even the general rule that sovereign immunity will not bar judicial relief against an officer for acts committed or threatened pursuant to an unconstitutional statute[6] and for acts *ultra vires*[7] but that it precludes relief where the challenged action is merely wrongful[8] is not altogether intelligible in terms of protecting the government in performing its essential functions. A like doubt applies to the distinction between affirmative and negative relief,[9] which has been an important determinant in judicial disposition of some immunity claims by public officers. The basis for the distinction has been the assumed need to protect executive and administrative officials in the exercise of their functions from undue interference by the judiciary, but the Court has failed to identify the need with any precision or to specify the countervailing considerations which account for exceptions to the principle and for the stratagems whereby it may be circumvented.[10]

Finally there is a conceptual rationale for sovereign immunity. In *Kawananakoa* v. *Polyblank* the Court, in a terse dictum by Justice Holmes, offered the following justification for the doctrine:

> Some doubts have been expressed as to the source of immunity of a sovereign power from suit without its own permission, but the answer has been public property since before the days of Hobbes. Leviathan, Chap. 26, 2. A sovereign is exempt from suit, not because of any formal conception or obsolete theory, but on the logical and practical ground that there can be no legal right as against the authority that makes the law on which the right depends. *"Car on*

peut bien recevoir loy d'autruy, mais il est impossible par nature de se donner loy." Bodin, Republique, 1, Chap. 8. . . .[11]

But for the eminence of its author, the statement surely would not have attracted much attention. Aside from the obvious criticism that the premise and the conclusion in this rationale are identical, Holmes' proposition is objectionable for postulating a conception of sovereignty that is even more authoritarian than the theory of kingship upon which the supremacy of the English ruler was based. As we have seen, the king was not regarded as being above the law and, hence, exempt from legal liability. His acts were simply beyond the purview of his own courts unless he agreed to submit to their jurisdiction. Holmes' rationale, if incongruent with English political and legal theory, is utterly incompatible with basic themes of American constitutionalism. The supreme authority that makes the law is the people in their constituent role. As against the people acting in this capacity there may be no legal right, but no exemption either from liability or amenability in favor of the state and government inheres in the ultimate sovereignty of the people. The principle, in fact, better points the other way.

The lack of a satisfactory rationale for the doctrine of sovereign immunity, and the tension between that doctrine and basic precepts of the American Constitution, account in large part for the erratic course traversed by the Court between 1873 and 1908 as immunity pleas by public officers were sustained or rejected in various cases. For all its importance, moreover, *Ex parte Young* did not provide a new dispensation. Although the opinion in that case brought to completion a major permutation in the interpretation of the Eleventh Amendment, the exemption of the states from federal judicial process survived, and the decisions since *Young,* even if generally less favorable to immunity pleas by public officers, have been unpredictable and as much enmeshed in legal casuistry as those of an earlier time.

In a 1964 brief submitted to the Court in *Griffin* v. *School Board of Prince Edward County,*[12] the attorney general of Virginia presented a twelve-page argument that the suit, brought to enjoin the school board, other agencies, and certain officers [13] from "refusing to maintain and operate an efficient system of public free schools," was a proceeding against the state barred by the Eleventh Amendment. To the attorney general's elaborate and well-documented argument, which was not adequately answered in the briefs of opposing counsel, the Court responded in a single sentence: "It has been settled law since *Ex parte Young* that suits against state and county officials to enjoin them from invading constitutional rights are not forbidden by the Eleventh Amendment."[14]

The Court's rejection in *Griffin* of the Eleventh Amendment defense is not at all surprising in the perspective of history. The amendment simply has not been much of an impediment to direct and immediate federal judicial relief in litigation challenging state policies of major social and economic significance. Broad control over state regulatory policies was asserted by the federal courts in the rate cases in spite of the amendment and in the face of an earlier construction which would have precluded direct judicial relief. At a later time, the amendment was to prove no more effective as an obstacle to judicially decreed desegregation and to reapportionment of the legislatures. Only at the periphery of such far-reaching issues has the Eleventh Amendment—and with respect to national policies, the immunity of the central government—been permitted to operate, precluding suits against the state and government *eo nomine* and, in suits against officers, inviting artifices designed to circumvent the sovereign's exemption from judicial process.

The Court's statement in *Griffin,* however, is startling for its brevity and exceptionable for what it passes over. Although *Ex parte Young* is good authority for the general proposition that state officers may be enjoined by the federal courts from violating constitutional rights, so too is practically every other case, beginning with *Osborn* v. *Bank of the United States,* in which officers asserted, whether successfully or not, immunity under the Eleventh Amendment. What the Court in *Griffin* failed to mention is that this general proposition is encumbered by exceptions and qualifications, the residue of precedents which *Ex parte Young* had not laid to rest and of some later expressions which *Young* did not anticipate. Nor would it have been necessary for the Court to have searched far back for these qualifications. Less than a year before its decision in *Griffin,* the Court had stated, in a unanimous *per curiam* opinion, that "the general rule is that relief sought nominally against an officer is in fact against the sovereign if the decree would operate against the latter."[15] And, in another unanimous opinion of the same term, the Court asserted that "the general rule is that a suit is against the sovereign 'if the judgment sought would expend itself on the public treasury or domain, or interfere with the public administration' or if the effect of the judgment would be 'to restrain the government from acting, or to compel it to act.' "[16] As statements of the "general rule" these expressions, which are similar to others in recent judicial opinions, are very inaccurate and misleading. The Court has often closed its eyes, quite deliberately, to the reality of whether a decree against an officer would operate against the government, as, in fact, it did in *Ex parte Young* and in later cases in which *Young* was followed. Moreover, some judgments against officers have expended themselves upon the public treasury or domain, more have interfered with the public administration, and a very large number have either restrained the government from acting or compelled it to act.[17] Still, however misleading these statements are as expressions of a general rule, they indicate that the law since *Ex parte Young* is not nearly as settled as the Court intimated in *Griffin;* moreover, they identify some persistent judicial concerns that account for the success of immunity pleas in certain cases.

The statement in *Griffin* simply bypassed substantial objections that the relief sought by the petitioner would require a levy of taxes and the expenditure of public money, that it would interfere with the public administration, and that it would simultaneously forbid the government from doing certain things while, in effect, commanding it to do other things.[18] To be sure, the petition was framed in the double negative—a familiar tactic to circumvent the perils of seeking an affirmative order—and it did not specifically demand the expenditure of public money. The Court, however, has repeatedly asserted that the nature of a suit as one against the state is to be determined "by the essential nature and effect of the proceeding, as it appears from the entire record."[19] In *Griffin* the Court refused to enter upon an analysis of this kind.

This is not to suggest that if such an analysis had been undertaken, the Court necessarily would have reached a conclusion unfavorable to the petitioner's claim. The general principles and rules the Court uses in disposing of immunity pleas by public officers are subject to numerous qualifications and exceptions and these in turn to other exceptions running back in favor of the general rules. Where one basis for extending or denying an exemption from judicial process is untenable, another may be advanced in support of a particular decision. A brief glance at a portion of the doctrinal terrain reveals the uncertainties: to the unsatisfactory and readily circumvented rule that affirmative relief will not be decreed against an officer[20] because it violates the immunity of the sovereign is the qualification that such relief may be allowed to compel the performance of a plain ministerial duty,[21] a qualification that has often deeply entangled the immunity doctrine in the traditional formalisms of the prerogative writs. But even if the duty to be performed is ministerial, involving no exercise of discretion, a judicial decree commanding disobedience to the positive orders of the supreme political power may be held to constitute an order against the sovereign.[22] Moreover, if the requested redress, whether affirmative or negative in form, would operate to divest the government of title to its property[23] or of money in its treasury,[24] the immunity of the sovereign may be successfully pleaded by the officer. Conversely, where title to the property and rights of possession are not in the government but in the complainant, the latter may obtain an order dispossessing the officer who occupies for the government,[25] but here too there is an important exception. An ejectment action against the officer infringes the immunity of the sovereign if an alternative remedy, such as a suit for damages, is open to the complainant.[26]

The legal sophistries employed by the Court in disposing of immunity claims and the uneven results achieved in such cases reflect the lack of a satisfactory rationale for the doctrine. They also express something of the ambivalence that judges experience in applying a doctrine that, as a matter of legal tradition, has been taken almost for granted but that is, by practically any standard, morally indefensible in modern society. As Justice Frankfurter remarked in his dissenting opinion in *Larson* v. *Domestic & Foreign Corporation:*

> The course of decisions concerning sovereign immunity is a good illustration of the conflicting considerations that often struggle for mastery in the judicial process, at least implicitly. In varying degrees, at different times, the momentum of the historic doctrine is arrested or deflected by an unexpressed feeling that governmental immunity runs counter to prevailing notions of reason and justice. Legal concepts are then found available to give effect to this feeling, and one of the results is the multitude of decisions in which this Court has refused to permit an agent of the government to claim that he is *pro tanto* the government and therefore sheltered by its immunity.[27]

The conflicting considerations to which Justice Frankfurter referred have left the case law defining sovereign immunity in disarray, and his efforts in this same opinion to explain and rationalize the results in previous cases going back to *Osborn*, while noteworthy, was not completely successful.[28] Nor can the decisions that followed *Young* or even those coming after *Larson* be reconciled upon the basis of any set of intelligible principles. [29] If anything, the exemption of the sovereign from suit through its officers, although somewhat weakened, is even less principled and more a matter of ad hoc determination than it was prior to the *Young* decision.

If, as has been suggested, the American doctrine of sovereign immunity is indefensible upon both theoretical and pragmatic grounds—if it represents, as the Court has more than once intimated, an unfortunate excrescence of a political and legal order which no longer enlists support—its continued observance should depend upon whether it is incorporated into the Constitution and hence made obligatory upon the judiciary unless waived by the government. It is clear enough, of course, that if the doctrine is to have constitutional status, it must be judicially inferred. There is absolutely nothing in the original Constitution nor in any of the amendments expressly sanctioning the doctrine. And to this generalization the Eleventh Amendment, despite the outcry about sovereign immunity and the sovereignty of the states which preceded its adoption, does not constitute an exception. That amendment, to be sure, did impose a limitation upon the federal judicial power with respect to suits brought against the states by certain classes of individuals, but its language does not support the Court's far-reaching statement that "as to the states, legal irresponsibility was written into the Eleventh Amendment."[30]

As an inference from the language of the judiciary article of the Constitution, the exemption of the sovereign from judicial process is of doubtful validity, as we have seen. When the general language of that article is read in the context of the broad purposes of the framers to maintain foreign peace and domestic harmony, as was repeatedly emphasized during the convention proceedings, and "to establish justice," as is stated in the preamble, the claim that the various delegations of judicial power generally were subject to the implied immunity of the sovereign from judicial process becomes unacceptable. Whether specific delegations should be regarded as qualified by this exemption is a more difficult problem, for distinctions are possible in terms of the purposes of the framers. Thus, an exemption in favor of the United States is at least arguable, as is the immunity of the states from suits by their own citizens under the federal-question clause, but as to these matters a firm judgment one way or the other would simply outrun available evidence.

Moreover, the proposal and the adoption of the Eleventh Amendment, even though with "vehement speed," does not constitute proof that the holding of the majority in *Chisholm* v. *Georgia* was constitutionally erroneous nor even that it was so regarded by those who drafted and ratified that instrument, notwithstanding later expressions of the Court to that effect. Between 1787 and 1794, the financial posture of the states toward their creditors significantly improved, so that the need for federal judicial remedies, apprehended at the time the Constitution was drafted, had substantially diminished. Still less does the text of the amendment and events attendant upon its adoption sustain the thesis that the various delegations of judicial power in Article III were generally qualified by the doctrine that a sovereign is exempt from suit, although this rationale appears in some opinions where exemptions not literally within the scope of the amendment were upheld.[31] At the time *Chisholm* was decided, there was a distinct possibility that the Court would similarly reject claims that other delegations of judicial power to the United States were implicitly qualified by the sovereign's exemption from suit. Even as to the immunity of the United States itself the several opinions in *Chisholm* were not entirely reassuring.[32] If Congress, in reacting to *Chisholm,* meant to confirm an implicit understanding that the grants of judicial power in Article III were delimited by the immunity doctrine, it chose, in proposing the Eleventh Amendment, singularly deficient language to convey that meaning.

Neither the text of the Eleventh Amendment nor the events

accounting for its adoption indicate that its principal purpose was to affirm or sanction the immunity of the sovereign. The amendment can be better understood as the constitutional outcome of the first in a protracted series of confrontations between the states, on the one hand, and the federal judiciary, on the other, over the nature of the Federal Union and the position of the states in the constitutional order. Although critics of *Chisholm* v. *Georgia* relied upon the immunity doctrine in challenging that decision, their primary concern was not with the immunity of the sovereign but with the sovereignty of the states. Subjection of the states to federal judicial process implied that they were not sovereign—a conclusion spelled out fully in the expansive rhetoric of the *Chisholm* majority.

With ratification of the Eleventh Amendment, the critics of *Chisholm* won quick reversal of the majority decision, but the victory was a very limited one. While the immediate grievance was eliminated by imposing a specific restriction upon the judicial power of the United States—exempting the states from suit in federal court by citizens of other states and by aliens—neither state sovereignty nor sovereign immunity was explicitly sanctioned. The amendment constituted little more than an exceedingly modest readjustment in national-state relations, and this, its federal aspect, was an important concern in the early Marshall court opinions. However, the federal theme of the amendment was generally overlooked in the state-officer cases of the late nineteenth century, as the amendment's restriction was uncritically equated with the abstract doctrine of sovereign immunity. The consequences of this development were, on the whole, mischievous. First, the immunity of the states from suits instituted by individuals in the national courts became virtually interchangeable with that of the United States from suit in its own tribunals, although the policy considerations lying behind the two exemptions are very different. Judicial attention was thereby deflected from meaningful inquiry whether, and in what circumstances, individuals with legal grievances against the states should enjoy direct access to the inferior federal courts for redress and relief. [33] Second, the identification of the Eleventh Amendment's prohibition with sovereign immunity, together with the equation of state immunity with that of the United States, had the effect of ascribing to the latter a constitutional legitimacy and a permanency altogether unwarranted.

The constitutional basis for the sovereign immunity doctrine in American law is extremely tenuous, and with respect to the immunity of the United States it may be no exaggeration to say that there is no demonstrable constitutional foundation at all, however firmly the exemption may be rooted in the legal tradition. State immunity is perhaps more securely based in the Constitution as a result of the Eleventh Amendment, but even so, the amendment, when understood as the constitutional resolution of a federal-state conflict, falls considerably short of permanently ensconcing the immunity of the states into the constitutional fabric.

There are, moreover, constitutional provisions that point toward repudiation rather than perpetuation of the immunity doctrine. If, as the Court has asserted, exempting the sovereign from enforceable legal responsibility conflicts with "expanding conceptions of public morality,"[34] there is a potential basis for renouncing the doctrine as violating the due-process guarantees of the Fifth and the Fourteenth amendments. Or, to put the matter in positive terms, due process may very well encompass an obligation of the states and the national government to afford the individual a means of legal redress in his relations with either. [35] "The claims of dominant opinion rooted in sentiments of justice and public morality," the Court has said, "are among the most powerful shaping-forces in lawmaking by the courts."[36] These forces have been important in delineating the broad and ambulatory contours of due process, especially where there is objective evidence that such sentiments are widely held and where, moreover, neither reason, expediency, nor a clear constitutional mandate can be marshaled the other way.

The absence of an adequate supporting rationale for the immunity doctrine, the unsatisfactory results that it has yielded, and its lack of solid constitutional underpinning already have been noticed. That the sentiment against it is widespread is evidenced by both national and state legislation waiving immunity from suit and enlarging governmental liability. In some states the judiciary has dealt the coup de grace, even in the face of state constitutional provisions explicitly sanctioning the doctrine.[37] Perpetuation of sovereign immunity elsewhere appears not to be due to any genuine conviction that it is useful but rather to legislative apathy and judicial timidity and attachment to *stare decisis.* And, where the doctrine survives, form has superseded substance as the courts have struggled to accommodate it with the rule of law.

Such an accommodation, perhaps, is not ultimately possible, nor is it desirable insofar as it compromises application of the rule of law to relations between the individual and government. Accommodation becomes unnecessary when the problem of interpretation is accurately perceived. Since the immunity of the national government rests upon a judicial inference rather than any explicit constitutional command, it may be withdrawn by judicial decision. With reference to the states, the prohibition upon the federal judicial power imposed by the Eleventh Amendment cannot be judicially abrogated, except as in many of the state officer cases—in essence but not in name. The amendment's restriction, however, is not equivalent to an affirmation of state immunity nor does it constitutionalize legal irresponsibility as a state's right. In this perspective, a judicial construction of due process of the Fourteenth Amendment imposing upon the states a constitutional obligation to provide effective means of legal redress for wrongs attributable to the states would present no direct conflict with the injunction of the Eleventh Amendment. It would, on the other hand, comport with deeply rooted sentiments about the just relationship between man and government, sentiments which found eloquent expression in *Chisholm* v. *Georgia* and which have been repeated, with continuing conviction, in ensuing years.

Notes

Chapter 1

1. *Chisholm* v. *Georgia,* 2 Dall. 419 (1793).

2. For a summary of the development of the common law during the early colonial period, see Paul S. Reinsch, *English Common Law in the Early American Colonies* (Madison: University of Wisconsin Bulletin No. 31, 1899), pp. 53-59. The influence of English law during the late colonial period is considered by Charles F. Mullett, *Fundamental Law and the American Revolution, 1760-1776* (New York: Octagon Books, 1966), pp. 33-78.

3. Richard B. Morris, *Studies in the History of American Law,* 2d ed. (New York: Octagon Books, 1964), pp. 67-68.

4. Edmund Burke, "Speech on Moving His Resolutions for Conciliation with the Colonies," (1775) in *Selected Writings of Edmund Burke,* ed. Walter J. Bate (New York: The Modern Library, 1960), pp. 126-127.

5. Sir William Holdsworth, *A History of English Law,* 3d ed. (London: Methuen & Co., 1944), IX, 8.

6. Literally, a manifestation of right, whereby a subject might, in order to obtain possession or restitution of property claimed by the crown, establish upon the basis of the record upon which the crown made claim, his own right. For a survey of the development of the *monstrans de droit* see Holdsworth, *History of English Law,* IX, 25-29.

7. In *Pawlett* v. *Attorney General,* Hardres 465, 145 Eng. Rep. 550 (Ex. 1668), the Court of Exchequer entertained a bill filed by a mortgagor to recover property that had escheated to the crown by reason of the mortgagee's attainder of treason. The *Bankers' Case,* 14 S.T. 1 (1690-1700)

involved proceedings instituted in the Court of Exchequer for payment of annuities owed by the crown out of hereditary revenues. A judgment in favor of the claimants, while reversed by the Exchequer Chamber, was subsequently sustained by the House of Lords. Long before the decisions in these cases, the Courts of Augmentations, Wards, and Surveyors had asserted jurisdiction over certain cases instituted by subjects against the king. As one authority stated, "the basic principle that the subject should of right be entitled to redress of grievance against the crown was recognized by statute, and process for the recovery of debts or money by the subject was a common occurrence in the Augmentations." See Walter C. Richardson, *History of the Court of Augmentations, 1536-1554* (Baton Rouge: Louisiana State University Press, 1961), p. 384.

8. See Holdsworth, *History of English Law*, IX, 15; Louis L. Jaffe, "Suits Against Governments and Officers," *Harvard Law Review*, 77 (1963): 4.

9. To this general principle, there were, no doubt, limited exceptions, particularly at an early time. See Ludwik Ehrlich, *Proceedings Against the Crown, 1216-1377*, Oxford Studies in Social and Legal History (Oxford: Clarendon Press, 1921), VI, 54ff.

10. Holdsworth, *History of English Law*, IX, 38-42.

11. Burke, "Resolutions for Conciliation," p. 127.

12. Sir William Blackstone, *Commentaries on the Laws of England* (Philadelphia: Robert Bell, Printer, 1770-1771), III, 254-255. See also I, 241-244.

13. However, the principle that the king can do no wrong subsequently had an important impact upon the *liability* of the sovereign for personal torts. As interpreted by the courts in the nineteenth century, this meant not only that the king himself was incapable of committing a tort but also that he could not authorize a servant to do so. Therefore, a tort committed by a subordinate was not imputable to the sovereign as it would be to anyone else. See Holdsworth, *History of English Law*, IX, 42-43.

14. *Ashby* v. *White*, 6 Mod. 45, 87 Eng. Rep. 808 (Q.B. 1702).

15. See Merrill Jensen, *The New Nation* (New York: Alfred A. Knopf, 1950), pp. 302-326, for a sympathetic account of financial policies pursued by the states during the Confederation period. Allan Nevins, *The American States During and After the Revolution* (New York: The Macmillan Co., 1927), pp. 541-543, emphasizes the progress of the states in retiring their debts.

16. Davis R. Dewey, *Financial History of the United States* (New York: Longmans Green & Co., 1934), pp. 56-57. See also Charles J. Bullock, *The Finances of the United States from 1775-1789*, University of Wisconsin Bulletin, Economics, Political Science and History Series, I, no. 2. (1895), p.

145; Albert S. Bolles, *The Financial History of the United States* (New York: D. Appleton and Co., 1892), I, 218-220.

17. B. U. Ratchford, *American State Debts* (Durham: Duke University Press, 1941), pp. 45-49.

18. See *Articles of Confederation,* Art. IX.

19. Alexander Hamilton to James Duane, September 3, 1780, in Henry Cabot Lodge, ed., *The Works of Alexander Hamilton* (New York and London: G. P. Putnam's Sons, 1904), I, 213-239.

20. Lodge, ed., *Works of Hamilton,* I, 305-306.

21. In February 1784, Hamilton appeared before the mayor's court of New York City as counsel for the defendant in the case of *Rutgers* v. *Waddington.* In this case, Elizabeth Rutgers brought suit for damages under the New York Trespass Act, which allowed people who had fled from the British army to recover damages from anyone who used the property during British occupation. Hamilton argued that damages should not be allowed upon the ground that the Treaty of Peace, which contained an amnesty provision, was superior to state law. The court did not, as is commonly supposed, clearly sustain Hamilton's contention, but it refused to award damages for the period of occupancy under British rule by construing the Trespass Act very narrowly.

22. Library of Congress, *Journals of the Continental Congress, 1774-1789* (Washington: Government Printing Office, 1934), XXXI, 494-498.

23. Ibid., p. 497.

24. James Madison to George Washington, April 16, 1787, in Department of State, *Documentary History of the Constitution* (Washington, 1894-1905), IV, 118.

25. See, for example, *Nathan* v. *Virginia,* 1 Dall. 77 (Court of Common Pleas, Philadelphia, 1784).

26. Ibid.

27. Thomas Sergeant, in "A Brief Sketch of the National Judiciary Powers" seems to imply that the Confederation would have had jurisdiction if Pennsylvania had failed to suppress the attachment. See Sergeant's comment in Peter S. Du Ponceau, *A Dissertation on the Jurisdiction of the Courts of the United States* (Philadelphia: Arthur Small, 1824), p. 157.

28. Among the fifteen resolutions introduced by Edmund Randolph, but generally believed to have been authored by Madison, was the following: "6. Resolved, that each branch ought to possess the right of originating acts; that the National Legislature ought to be empowered to enjoy the legislative rights vested in Congress by the Confederation, and moreover *to legislate in all cases to which the separate States are incompetent, or in which the*

*harmony of the United States may be interrupted by the exercise of indi-
vidual legislation; to negative all laws passed by the several States contraven-
ing, in the opinion of the National Legislature, the Articles of Union or any
treaty subsisting under the authority of the Union. . . .*" James Madison,
Journal of the Federal Convention, ed. E. H. Scott (Chicago: Scott, Foresman
and Co., 1898), I, 62. (Italics mine.)

29. "Notes on the Confederacy" (April 1787), in James Madison, *Letters
and Other Writings,* ed. Philip R. Fendall (Philadelphia: J. B. Lippincott and
Co., 1867), I, 321. See also James Madison "Introduction to the Debates in
the Convention" in *Journal of the Federal Convention,* I, 47.

30. "No State shall . . . coin money; emit Bills of Credit; make any Thing
but gold and silver Coin a Tender in Payment of Debts; pass any . . . Law
impairing the Obligation of Contracts." U.S., *Constitution,* Art. I, sec. 10.

31. Madison, *Journal,* I, 62-63. (Italics mine.) On the same day, Charles
Pinckney of South Carolina presented a plan of government, which included a
judiciary article providing for the jurisdiction of the federal courts as follows:
"The judges of the courts shall hold their offices during good behaviour; and
receive a compensation, which shall not be increased or diminished during
their continuance in office. One of these courts shall be termed the Supreme
Court; whose jurisdiction shall extend to all cases arising under the laws of
the United States, or affecting ambassadors, other public ministers and
consuls; to the trial of impeachment of officers of the United States; to all
cases of admiralty and maritime jurisdiction. In cases of impeachment affecting ambassadors, and other public ministers, this jurisdiction shall be original;
and in all other cases appellate." Ibid., p. 70.

32. "By questions involving 'the national peace and harmony' no one can
suppose more was meant than might be *specified,* by the Convention as
proper to be referred to the Judiciary either, by the Constitution or Constitutional authority of the Legislature. They could be no rule, in that latitude, to
a Court, nor even to a Legislature with limited powers." This is a paragraph
from a letter by Madison, apparently not sent, in reply to a speech of John
Tyler delivered on February 6, 1833. Department of State, *Documentary
History of the Constitution,* V, 386.

33. Madison, *Journal,* I, 157.

34. Ibid.

35. As amended, the clause then read: "cases in which foreigners, or
citizens of two distinct states of the Union, applying to such jurisdictions,
may be interested. . . ."

36. Madison, *Journal,* I, 157.

37. Ibid., pp. 165-166. The Paterson plan was laid before the convention
on June 15.

38. Ibid., p. 186. The Hamilton plan, presented as a sketch of his ideas and not as a formal proposal, was laid before the convention on June 18.

39. Ibid., p. 379.

40. Ibid., II, 449.

41. The committee's working papers are among the Wilson Papers in the Library of the Historical Society of Pennsylvania, and they are printed, together with related source materials, in Max Farrand, *The Records of the Federal Convention* (New Haven: Yale University Press, 1911), II, 129-175.

42. Ibid., p. 147.

43. Ibid. There is also added, again in the handwriting of Rutledge, the clause "and in cases of admiralty jurisdiction."

44. Ibid., pp. 173-174.

45. Madison, *Journal*, II, 458-459. (Italics mine.)

46. U.S., *Constitution*, Art. III, sec. 2.

47. See the opinions of Justices Blair and Cushing in *Chisholm* v. *Georgia*, 2 Dall. 419 (1793).

48. The first case upholding an immunity plea by the United States was *United States* v. *McLemore*, 4 How. 286 (1846), but there were earlier dicta to this effect. *Cohens* v. *Virginia*, 6 Wheat. 264, 411-412 (1821).

49. See Jonathan Elliot, ed., *The Debates in the Several State Conventions on the Adoption of the Federal Constitution* (Philadelphia: J. B. Lippincott and Co., 1876), III, 207, 573-574.

50. *Vanstophorst* v. *Maryland*, 2 Dall. 401 (1791).

51. *Chisholm* v. *Georgia*, 2 Dall. 419 (1793).

52. See Elliot, *Debates*, II, 491.

53. "That all courts shall be open, and every man, for an injury done him in his lands, goods, person, or reputation, shall have remedy by the due course of law, and right and justice administered without sale, denial, or delay. Suits may be brought against the commonwealth in such manner, in such courts, and in such cases as the legislature may by law direct." Constitution of Pennsylvania (1790), Article IX, sec. 11. For an indication of Wilson's views on the suability of states, see James D. Andrews, ed., *The Works of James Wilson* (Chicago: Callaghan and Co., 1896), II, 151-153. Wilson's views on the matter of the suability of the states led one commentator to suggest that Wilson was the author of the constitutional clause extending the judicial power to controversies between states and citizens of other states. See Allen C. Braxton, "The Eleventh Amendment," *Virginia State Bar Association Report* 20 (1907), 175.

54. See below, pp. 41-43, for an analysis of pertinent provisions of the Judiciary Act of 1789, which Ellsworth authored.

Chapter 2

1. For materials and comment on criticisms of the proposed Constitution, see Cecelia M. Kenyon, ed., *The Antifederalists* (Indianapolis: The Bobbs-Merrill Co., 1966), and Jackson T. Main, *The Antifederalists* (Chapel Hill: University of North Carolina Press, 1961).

2. Before the convention assembled, sixteen members of the Pennsylvania assembly who had opposed legislative action calling the convention issued an address to the people, which included the following warning: "You will be able, likewise, to determine whether in a free government, there ought or ought not to be any provision against a standing army in time of peace? or whether the trial by jury in civil causes is becoming dangerous and ought to be abolished? and whether the judiciary of the United States is not so constructed as to absorb and destroy the judiciaries of the several States? You will also be able to judge whether such inconveniencies have been experienced by the present mode of trial between citizen and citizen of different States as to render a continental court necessary for that purpose? or whether there can be any real use in the appellate jurisdiction with respect to fact as well as law?" John B. McMaster and Frederick D. Stone, eds., *Pennsylvania and the Federal Constitution, 1787-1788* (Philadelphia: Historical Society of Pennsylvania, 1888), p. 78. In reply to this address Pelatiah Webster wrote his "Remarks on the Address of Sixteen Members of the Assembly of Pennsylvania" in which he said: "I do not find one article of the constitution proposed, which vests congress, or any of their officers or courts, with a power to interfere in the least in the internal police or government of any one state, when the interests of some other state or strangers, or the union in general, are not concerned. ... I answer, both the original and appellate jurisdiction of the federal judiciary are manifestly necessary, where the cause of action affects the citizens of different states, the general interest of the union, or strangers (and to cases of these descriptions only, does the jurisdiction of the federal judiciary extend). . . ." Ibid., pp. 99, 102.

3. "But when a dispute arises between the citizens of any state about lands lying out of the bounds thereof, or when a trial is to be had between the citizens of any state and those of another, or the government of another, the private citizen will not be obliged to go into a court constituted by the state, with which, or with the citizens of which, his dispute is. He can appeal to a disinterested federal court. This is surely a great advantage, and promises a fair trial, and an impartial judgment." Tench Coxe, "An Examination of the Constitution," p. 17, in Paul L. Ford, *Pamphlets on the Constitution, 1787-1788* (Brooklyn, 1888).

4. Jonathan Elliot, ed., *The Debates in the Several State Conventions on the Adoption of the Federal Constitution* (Philadelphia: J. B. Lippincott and Co., 1876), II, 491-492.

5. McMaster and Stone, *Pennsylvania and the Constitution*, p. 423.

6. The defeated amendment was as follows: "14. That the judiciary power of the United States shall be confined to cases affecting ambassadors, other public ministers, and consuls, to cases of admiralty and maritime jurisdiction, to controversies to which the United States shall be a party, to controversies between two or more States—between a State and citizens of different States—between citizens claiming lands under grants of different States, and between a State or the citizens thereof and foreign States, and in criminal cases, to such only as are enumerated in the constitution, and that the United States in Congress assembled, shall not have power to enact laws, which shall alter the laws of descents and distributions on the effects of deceased persons, the title of land or goods, or the regulation of contracts in the individual States." Ibid.

7. See Elliot, *Debates*, II, 109-110.

8. Ibid., p. 177. The seventh proposal of amendment was: "The Supreme judicial Federal Court shall have no jurisdiction of causes between citizens of different states, unless the matter in dispute, whether it concern the realty or personalty, be of the value of three thousand dollars at the least; nor shall the federal judicial powers extend to any action between citizens of different states, where the matter in dispute, whether it concern the realty or personalty, is not of the value of fifteen hundred dollars at the least." The New Hampshire convention proposed the same amendment. See U.S., Department of State, *Documentary History of the Constitution* (Washington, 1894-1905), II, 143.

9. William V. Wells, *The Life and Public Services of Samuel Adams* (Boston: Little, Brown, and Co., 1865), III, 330-331.

10. Samuel B. Harding, *The Contest over the Ratification of the Federal Constitution in the State of Massachusetts* (New York: Longmans, Green, and Co., 1896), pp. 40-41.

11. Sullivan to Rufus King, September 28, 1787, in Charles R. King, *The Life and Correspondence of Rufus King* (New York: G. P. Putnam's Sons, 1894), I, 260. See also, Harding, *Contest over Ratification*, p. 41.

12. See Harding, *Contest over Ratification*, pp. 21-22.

13. Agrippa Letter No. V, *Massachusetts Gazette*, December 11, 1787, reprinted in Paul L. Ford, ed., *Essays on the Constitution* (Brooklyn: Historical Printing Club, 1892), p. 67.

14. Ibid.

15. Ibid.

16. Agrippa Letter No. XIII, *Massachusetts Gazette,* January 14, 1788, in Ford, ed., *Essays,* p. 97.

17. Ibid., p. 99. See also Agrippa Letter No. XVIII, *Massachusetts Gazette,* February 5, 1788, in Ford, ed., *Essays,* pp. 118-119.

18. Pickering to Charles Tillinghast, draft, December 24, 1787, in Charles W. Upham, *The Life of Timothy Pickering* (Boston: Little, Brown, and Co., 1873), II, 336.

19. Elliot, *Debates,* III, 207.

20. Ibid., pp. 318-319.

21. Ibid., pp. 475-476.

22. Ibid., pp. 476-577.

23. Ibid., pp. 517-518. See also Pendleton's defense of the article, p. 549.

24. Ibid., pp. 526-527.

25. The Indiana Company, whose shareholders were mostly Pennsylvania citizens, claimed 3 million acres of western land under an Indian conveyance. The state of Virginia refused to recognize this claim, and treated the tract as public land of the state.

26. Ibid., pp. 529-530.

27. Ibid., p. 533.

28. Ibid., pp. 543-544.

29. Ibid.

30. Ibid., p. 555.

31. Ibid., p. 556. See also his remarks, pp. 557-558.

32. Ibid., p. 573.

33. Ibid., p. 574.

34. An attempt to make the amendments a condition of ratification was defeated, 88 to 80. Ibid., p. 653.

35. Ibid., pp. 660-661.

36. The resolution of ratification, together with recommended amendments, passed by a vote of 89 to 79.

37. Technically, the Constitution became effective with ratification by the ninth state, New Hampshire. It was widely recognized, however, that approval by Virginia and New York would be necessary to the success of the new government.

38. Richard Henry Lee, *Observations Leading to a Fair Examination of the System of Government Proposed by the Late Convention (Letters of a Federal Farmer)* (1787) reprinted, in Ford, *Pamphlets.*

39. Ibid., p. 31.

40. Alexander Hamilton, John Jay, and James Madison, *The Federalist,* No. 81 (New York: The Modern Library, n.d.), pp. 529-530.

41. The New York convention, by a vote of 31 to 29, had earlier refused to approve a motion which would have limited the state's obligations under the new government until a second convention of the states was called to consider amendments. Elliot, *Debates*, II, 411-412.

42. Department of State, *Documentary History of the Constitution*, II, 194. See also Elliot, *Debates*, II, 409. (Italics mine.)

43. These objections reechoed those of George Mason, as stated in "The Objections of the Honorable George Mason" in Ford, *Pamphlets*. James Iredell (Marcus) wrote, in reply, his "Answers to Mr. Mason's Objections to the Constitution," also in Ford, *Pamphlets*.

44. Elliot, *Debates*, IV, 159.

45. Ibid., pp. 248-251.

46. Ibid., p. 246.

47. Ibid., p. 247.

48. Department of State, *Documentary History of the Constitution*, II, 317. See also William R. Staples, *Rhode Island in the Continental Congress* (Providence: Providence Press Co., 1870), p. 656; and Frank G. Bates, *Rhode Island and the Formation of the Union*, Columbia University Studies in History, Economics, and Public Law, X, no. 2 (New York: Macmillan Co., 1898), pp. 205-206.

Chapter 3

1. Portions of this chapter were previously published in my "Prelude to Amendment: The States Before the Court," *The American Journal of Legal History* 12 (January 1968), 19-40.

2. An Act to Establish the Judicial Courts of the United States, Section 13, c. 20, 1 Stat. 80 (1789) (Italics mine.)

3. See below, pp. 96-97. For a discussion of changes in the original committee bill, See Charles Warren, "New Light on the Federal Judiciary Act of 1789," *Harvard Law Review*, 37 (November 1923), 49-132.

4. Act to Establish Judicial Courts, 1 Stat. 80. (Italics mine.)

5. Under Section 9 the district courts "shall also have cognizance, concurrent as last mentioned, of all suits at common law where the United States sue, and the matter in dispute amounts, exclusive of costs, to the sum or value of one hundred dollars." Ibid., 1 Stat. 77. Section 11 provided that "the circuit courts shall have original cognizance, concurrent with the courts of the several states, of all suits of a civil nature at common law or in equity, where the matter in dispute exceeds, exclusive of costs, the sum or value of five hundred dollars, and the United States are plaintiffs, or petitioners." Ibid., 1 Stat. 78.

6. *Vanstophorst* v. *Maryland,* 2 Dall. 401 (1791). This case is variously entitled *Van Stophorst* or *Van Staphorst* v. *Maryland.* The records in Dallas are fragmentary and inaccurate, and several of the early cases are not reported at all. Much of the factual material concerning these cases was taken from the official minutes and dockets of the Supreme Court.

7. See Hugh S. Hanna, *A Financial History of Maryland,* Johns Hopkins Univerity Studies in Historical and Political Science, XXV (Baltimore: The Johns Hopkins Press, 1907), pp. 19, 30.

8. Minutes of the Supreme Court of the United States, February 8, 1791.

9. Ibid., August 3, 1791.

10. Ibid., August 6, 1792. The settlement was reached in 1793. See Hanna, *Financial History,* p. 30.

11. For references to some newpaper comment on the case, see Charles Warren, *The Supreme Court in United States History* (Boston: Little, Brown, and Co., 1937), I, 92n2.

12. James Sullivan, *Observations upon the Government of the United States of America* (Boston: Samuel Hall, 1791); Hortensius, *An Enquiry into the Constitutional Authority of the Supreme Federal Court over the Several States in Their Political Capacity* (Charleston: W. P. Young, 1792). The second essay was for many years attributed to David Ramsay; recent scholarship ascribes it to Timothy Ford.

13. *Oswald* v. *New York,* 2 Dall. 401 (1792). The facts of *Oswald* v. *New York* were not reported by Dallas. The background of the case has been reconstructed from the *Oswald* v. *New York* case file in the National Archives. The file is incomplete, however, and many of the documents were badly damaged by fire.

14. The case provides some interesting evidence of contemporaneous standards of judicial conduct. Chief Justice Jay did not disqualify himself, although as a member of the New York convention, he had participated in the decision to employ Holt, a fact to which he swore in a 1794 affidavit filed at Oswald's request. National Archives, Supreme Court of the United States Case File, *Oswald* v. *New York,* 1792-1795.

15. Minutes of the Supreme Court, February 11, 1792.

16. Ibid., February 14, 1792.

17. Ibid., August 6, 1792.

18. Ibid., August 7, 1792.

19. On January 8, 1794, Governor Clinton delivered an address before a joint session of the legislature. He made the following statement: "Among many other important matters, which will occupy your deliberations, are certain resolutions of the Legislature of Massachusetts and Virginia, respect-

ing the suability of a state: which are submitted to you at the request of the executives of those commonwealths. The decision of the Supreme Federal Court, which gave rise to these resolves, involves so essentially the sovereignty of each state, that no observations on my part can be necessary to bespeak your early attention to the subject matter of them. It may be proper, however, to suggest that our Convention, when deliberating the Federal Constitution, in order to prevent the judiciary of the United States from attending itself to questions of this nature, expressly guarded against such a construction by their instrument of ratification. A suit has, notwithstanding, been instituted by an individual against this state. To you, therefore, it will belong to pursue such measures as the occasion may require, consistent with the constitution of the United States, and best corresponding with our own sovereignty, and the general welfare of the Union." *Journal of the Assembly of the State of New York,* 17th sess., January-March 1794, p. 7.

20. Ibid., p. 17.

21. *Journal of the Senate of the State of New York,* January-March 1794, p. 10.

22. *Journal of the Assembly,* 17th sess., p. 39. The assembly declined to concur in a senate resolution calling for a constitutional amendment because such a proposal had already been approved by the Senate of the United States and action upon it was pending in the House of Representatives.

23. During its first years, the Supreme Court routinely, at the beginning of each term, drew a jury list, and in at least three cases a jury was impaneled and a verdict rendered: *Oswald* v. *New York,* Minutes of the Supreme Court, February 5-6, 1795; *Georgia* v. *Brailsford,* Minutes of the Supreme Court, February 5, 1794; *Cutting* v. *South Carolina,* Minutes of the Supreme Court, August 8, 1797.

24. Minutes of the Supreme Court, February 6, 1795.

25. *Chisholm* v. *Georgia,* 2 Dall. 419 (1793); *Grayson* v. *Virginia,* 3 Dall. 320 (1796), later decided as *Hollingsworth* v. *Virginia,* 3 Dall. 378 (1798); and *Vassall* v. *Massachusetts* (unreported case, docketed in August 1793).

26. *Chisholm* v. *Georgia,* 2 Dall. 419.

27. Earlier misconceptions about *Chisholm* v. *Georgia* are dispelled by Doyle Mathis, "Chisholm v. Georgia: Background and Settlement," *Journal of American History* 54 (June 1967), 19-29.

28. Ibid., p. 22.

29. *Farquhar's Executor* v. *Georgia* (1791), an unreported case. The case file is among the Records of the United States Circuit Court, Georgia District.

30. *Farquhar's Executor* v. *Georgia,* Case File.

31. Mathis, "Chisholm v. Georgia," p. 22-16, suggests that it is erroneous to consider *Chisholm* v. *Georgia* as an original case in the Supreme Court of

the United States. While it is true that the case originated in the circuit court, Chisholm did not sue out a writ of error from the decision of the circuit court dismissing the suit. He filed an original suit in the Supreme Court.

32. Minutes of the Supreme Court, August 11, 1792.

33. *Chisholm* v. *Georgia*, 2 Dall. 419. The governor had requested the legislature to take cognizance of the suit as early as December 1792, and a resolution of protest was introduced in the lower chamber. *Augusta Chronicle and Gazette*, December 22, 1792. The resolution did not pass, however, and Georgia's remonstrance was by authority of the governor.

34. *Chisholm* v. *Georgia*, 2 Dall. 419.

35. Ibid., 422.

36. Ibid., 423.

37. Ibid., 424-425. Randolph emphasized, however, that the United States could not be sued either in state or federal courts. In the one instance this would make the head of the confederacy subject to the courts of inferior members, and in the other a sovereign would be subjected to his own courts.

38. Ibid., 426-427.

39. The other questions were: "(2) If the state of Georgia can be made a party defendant in certain cases, does an action of *assumpsit* lie against her? (3) Is the service of the summons upon the governor and attorney general of the state of Georgia, a competent service? (4) By what process ought the appearance of the state of Georgia to be enforced?" Ibid., 420.

40. Minutes of the Supreme Court, February 5, 1793.

41. The membership of the Court was fixed at six, but shortly before the case was argued, Justice Thomas Johnson resigned, and his successor, William Paterson, had not yet been appointed.

42. *Chisholm* v. *Georgia*, 2 Dall. 419, 430. For an analysis of Iredell's opinion, see Jeff B. Fordham, "Iredell's Dissent in Chisholm v. Georgia," *North Carolina Historical Review* 7 (1931), 155.

43. *Chisholm* v. *Georgia*, 2 Dall. 432-434.

44. Ibid., 449-450.

45. Ibid., 453. Wilson had already suggested his answer in a lecture at the University of Pennsylvania when he asserted, "In controversies, to which the state or nation is a party, the state or nation itself ought to be amenable before the judicial powers." He indicated that even the United States may be amenable to suit. See James Wilson, *The Works of James Wilson*, ed. James D. Andrews (Chicago: Callaghan and Co., 1896), II, 151-152.

46. *Chisholm* v. *Georgia*, 2 Dall. 419, 455.

47. Ibid., 461.

48. Ibid., 470.

49. Ibid., 470-471.

50. *Georgia* v. *Brailsford,* 2 Dall. 402 (1792). See *n.* 56, below.

51. *Chisholm* v. *Georgia,* 2 Dall. 419, 476.

52. Ibid., 477. The Chief Justice's holding that a state is suable by a citizen of another state was not unequivocal, however. At the end of his opinion he asserted that there might be exceptions: "I am far from being prepared to say that an individual may sue a state on bills of credit issued before the Constitution was established, and which were issued and received on the faith of the state, and at a time when no ideas or expectations of judicial interposition were entertained or contemplated." Ibid., 479.

53. On August 5, 1793, Alexander J. Dallas and Jared Ingersoll, "by virtue of an authority from the State of Georgia," appeared to show cause why a default judgment should not be entered, and on the following day the parties consented to a continuance of the case until February 1794. The Minutes of the Supreme Court, under February 14, 1794, disclose that the Court heard Dallas and Ingersoll, and then voted unanimously (with Justice Iredell absent) to enter a judgment in favor of the plaintiff. At this time, on motion of Attorney General Randolph, a writ of enquiry to ascertain damages was awarded. On August 5, 1794, again on Randolph's motion, the Court directed that the jury to be summoned at the February 1795 term make a finding on the damages to which the plaintiff was entitled.

54. See Mathis, "Chisholm v. Georgia," p. 27. In settlement of the claim, Georgia issued to Farquhar's heir audited certificates in the amount of £7,586. This sum approximated the £63,605 in South Carolina currency of 1777, the amount originally due.

55. For comment in newspapers of the time, see Warren, *Supreme Court in United States History,* I, 96-99. See also Charles Page Smith, *James Wilson* (Chapel Hill: University of North Carolina Press, 1956), p. 358.

56. *The Augusta Chronicle,* November 9, 1793, reporting the governor's message of November 6.

The state of Georgia apparently did not regard an appearance as plaintiff before the Court as posing the same dangers. *Georgia* v. *Brailsford,* 2 Dall. 402, 415, (1792, 1793), 3 Dall. 1 (1794), grew out of a suit by a British creditor against a citizen of Georgia in a federal circuit court, *Brailsford* v. *Spalding* (unreported). Georgia claimed title to the property in question and sought to intervene in the suit. When the circuit court refused to admit the state as a party, Georgia filed in the Supreme Court an original bill in equity to enjoin execution of the circuit court's judgment in favor of the creditor. In 1792, the Supreme Court granted a temporary injunction, and, the following year, after full argument, the Court ruled that the state's remedy was at law, although the injunction was continued until the following year. Suit was joined in 1794, and a jury rendered a verdict in favor of the defendant.

57. *The Augusta Chronicle,* November 16, 1793, reporting the action of November 9.

58. Ibid., November 23, 1793, reporting the action of November 19.

59. *Moultrie* v. *Georgia, Cutting* v. *South Carolina.*

60. Docket of the Supreme Court, February Term, 1793. The case appears to have been instituted with service of a complaint in August 1792. See Sherwin McRae, ed., *Calendar of Virginia State Papers* (Richmond: A. R. Micon, 1886), VI, 1. An aspect of the case is reported in 3 Dall. 320 (1796).

61. The case was eventually dismissed, after ratification of the Eleventh Amendment, *sub nom.* *Hollingsworth* v. *Virginia,* 3 Dall. 378 (1798). Warren, *Supreme Court in United States History,* I, 92n1, 99n2, incorrectly implies that the *Indiana Company* and *Grayson* cases were separate actions.

62. Important documentary material bearing upon the case is collected in McRae, ed., *Calendar of Virginia State Papers,* VI, 1-36.

63. See George Mason to Roger West, November 9, 1791, in Kate Mason Rowland, *The Life of George Mason* (New York: G. P. Putnam's Sons, 1892), II, 342-345.

64. Ibid., 345.

65. Attorney General James Innes to Governor Henry Lee, January 22, 1793, in McRae, ed., *Calendar of Virginia State Papers,* VI, 26.

66. Governor Henry Lee to Lieutenant Governor James Wood, March 3, 1793, in McRae, ed., *Calendar of Virginia State Papers,* VI, 301.

67. George Mason to Roger West, November 9, 1791, in Rowland, *Life of George Mason,* II, 344.

68. For the text of these resolutions, adopted December 3, 1793, see *Journal of the House of Delegates of Virginia,* Session of October 21, 1793, p. 99.

69. Minutes of the Supreme Court, March 14, 1796.

70. Ibid., August 12, 1796.

71. *Hollingsworth* v. *Virginia,* 3 Dall. 378 (1798).

72. Docket of the Supreme Court, August Term, 1793; Minutes of the Supreme Court, August 6, 1793.

73. See Herbert S. Allan, *John Hancock* (New York: Beechhurst Press, 1953), 357-358.

74. *The Augusta Chronicle,* November 2, 1793.

75. Ibid.

76. Ibid.

77. Resolution of the General Court of Massachusetts, September 27, 1793, in Allan, *John Hancock,* pp. 357-358.

78. Minutes of the Supreme Court, February 13, 1797.

79. Minutes of the Supreme Court, February 1796. The case is mentioned by Charles Warren as *Catlin* v. *South Carolina*. See Warren, *Supreme Court in United States History*, I, 104n2.

80. *Journal of the House of Representatives of South Carolina*, Session of November 1796, pp. 54-55.

81. Minutes of the Supreme Court, August 8, 1797.

82. Many years later, in *Monaco* v. *Mississippi*, 292 U.S. 313 (1934), the Court held that the judicial power of the United States under Art. III, sec. 2, of the Constitution did not extend to suits instituted against a nonconsenting state by a foreign state or sovereign.

83. Docket of the Supreme Court, February 1797 term. An aspect of the case is reported in Dallas under the title *Huger* v. *South Carolina*, 3 Dall. 339 (1797). The complainants' bill is in U.S., Congress, *American State Papers, I: Public Lands* (Washington: Gales and Seaton, 1832), pp. 167-171.

84. See C. Peter Magrath, *Yazoo: Law and Politics in the New Republic* (Providence: Brown University Press, 1966), pp. 4-5. This second sale was effected through widespread bribery of legislators, and its attempted rescission the following year set the stage for *Fletcher* v. *Peck*, 6 Cranch 87 (1810).

85. On August 18, 1789, Representative Thomas Tucker of South Carolina introduced a series of amendments to the Constitution. Among his proposals was one "to strike from Article III, section 2, the words 'between a State and citizens of another State,' etc. to the end, and to amend to read thus: 'between a State and foreign States, and between citizens of the United States claiming the same lands under grants of different States.' " The House rejected a motion to refer these amendments to the Committee of the Whole for consideration. *Annals of Congress* (1st Cong., 1st Sess., August 18, 1789), I, 762-763.

86. Ibid. (2d Cong., February 20, 1793), III, 651-652. Herman V. Ames attributes authorship of this proposal to Theodore Sedgwick of Massachusetts, but Sedgwick was a member of the House and not of the Senate. See his *Proposed Amendments to the Constitution*, App. no. 313.

87. *Journal of the Senate of North Carolina* (December 1793), pp. 35-36. The Connecticut resolution does not appear in the fragmentary records of that state's legislature, but see *Catalogue of Documents and Papers of the Senate of Massachusetts*, I, 143, for a reference to the Connecticut resolution.

88. The New Hampshire resolution declared "that in the opinion of this Convention, the Senators from this State in the Congress of the United States be instructed, and the representatives requested to use their utmost endeavors to obtain at their present session, such amendments in the Constitution of the United States, as to prevent the possibility of a construction which may

justify a decision that a State is compellable to the suit of an individual or individuals in the Courts of the United States." *Journal of the Proceedings of the Honorable House of Representatives of the State of New Hampshire* (December 1793), pp. 110-117.

89. See *Journal of the Assembly of the State of New York* (17th session, January 1794) pp. 7, 16-17, 21, 29, 39-40; *Votes and Proceedings of the House of Delegates of the State of Maryland* (November 1793), pp. 115-116, 123: *Journal of the Senate of South Carolina* (November 1793), ibid., (December 17, 18, 1793). Proceedings in Georgia are reported in *The Augusta Chronicle*, November 15, 19, 21, 1793.

90. *Journal of the First Session of the Fourth House of Representatives of Pennsylvania* (December 1793), pp. 61-62.

91. *Journal of the Senate of the State of Delaware* (January 1794), p. 9.

92. *Annals of Congress* (3d Cong., January 2, 1794), IV, 25.

93. Ibid. (January 14, 1794), IV, 30.

94. Ibid. (March 4, 1794), pp. 476-477.

95. *Journal of the Assembly of the State of New York* (17th sess., January 1794), pp. 177-178. Legislative action approving the amendment appears to have been completed on March 27, 1794.

96. Rhode Island appears to have ratified in March or April 1794 (*Journal of the House of Magistrates*, 1794), but President Washington did not transmit notice to Congress until January 29, 1796. James D. Richardson, ed., *Messages of the Presidents* (Washington: Bureau of National Literature, 1912), I, 182. Connecticut: May 14, 1794 (*Records of the States of the United States*). New Hampshire: June 16, 1794 (*Journals of the Senate of New Hampshire,* 1794), p. 40. Massachusetts: June 14, 1794 (*Journal of the House of Representatives* [15th sess.], p. 102). Vermont: October 28, 1794 (*Journal of Proceedings of the General Assembly,* 1794, p. 179). Virginia: November 18, 1794 (*Journal of the House of Delegates,* 1794, p. 20). Georgia: November 29, 1794 (*Executive Department Minutes,* in Julia M. Bland, *Georgia and the Federal Constitution* [Washington: Department of State Publication 1078, 1937], pp. 16-18). Kentucky: December 8, 1794 (*Journal of the House of Representatives,* 1794, p. 34). Maryland: December 26, 1794 (*Votes and Proceedings of the Senate of the State of Maryland,* 1794, p. 52). Delaware: January 30, 1795 (*Journal of the House of Representatives,* 1795, p. 52). North Carolina: February 7, 1795 (*Journal of the House of Commons,* 1794-1795, p. 38). In some of the states approval of ratification bills required the subsequent assent of the governor.

97. In most states the vote was not recorded. In Maryland, the vote in the lower chamber was 50 to 4, but in the senate, 6 to 5. In New York, the vote

was 49 to 2 in the house, with no record vote in the senate. The New Hampshire house voted 92 to 14 in favor of the amendment. The Virginia House of Delegates approved unanimously.

98. In a message dated January 8, 1798, President Adams transmitted "a report of the Secretary of State, with a copy of an act of the legislature of Kentucky consenting to the ratification of the amendment of the Constitution of the United States proposed by Congress in their resolution of the 2d day of December, 1793, relative to the suability of States." See Richardson, *Messages and Papers of the President*, I, 250. The carelessness which characterized the whole process is revealed by Adams' failure to ascertain even the correct date of the proposal.

99. South Carolina: December 4, 1797 (*Journal of the Senate*, 1797, p. 68). In Pennsylvania the records disclose no legislative action after the governor transmitted the proposed amendment on March 21, 1794 (*Journal of the House of Representatives*, 1794, pp. 274-276). Opposition appears to have been strong in Pennsylvania, the only state at that time permitting suits against the state by individuals in its own courts. Pennsylvania, *Constitution* (1790), Art. IX, sec. 11. Records of the New Jersey legislature for this period are unavailable, but a letter from the secretary of state of New Jersey, August 20, 1797, in the State Department Manuscript Archives indicates that the amendment was not ratified. Tennessee was admitted to the Union in 1796. Secretary of State Pickering certified the proposed amendment to the governor of Tennessee in October 1797, and there is no record of legislative action, possibly because ratification by the requisite number of states was formally announced only a short time later.

100. See Charles G. Haines, *The Role of the Supreme Court in American Government and Politics, 1789-1835* (Berkeley: University of California Press, 1944), p. 138; Ulrich P. Phillips, *Georgia and State Rights* (Annual Report of the American Historical Association, 1901), II, 28; Karl Singewald, *The Doctrine of Non-Suability of the State in the United States*, Johns Hopkins University Studies in Historical and Political Science, Series XXVIII, no. 3 (Baltimore: Johns Hopkins Press, 1910), pp. 18-19. Judicial comment to the same effect occurs in *Hans* v. *Louisiana*, 134 U.S. 1, 11-15 (1890) and in *Larson* v. *Domestic & Foreign Corporation*, 337 U.S. 682, 708 (1949).

101. See, for example, Louis L. Jaffe, "Suits Against Governments and Officers: Sovereign Immunity," *Harvard Law Review* 77 (November 1963), 19. There are judicial statements to this effect in *Missouri* v. *Fiske*, 290 U.S. 18, 27 (1933), and *Petty* v. *Tennessee-Missouri Bridge Commission*, 359 U.S. 275 (1959).

102. U.S., Congress, *American State Papers, I: Finance,* pp. 28-29.

103. B. U. Ratchford, *American State Debts* (Durham: Duke University Press, 1941), p. 60.

104. Ibid., pp. 68-72.

105. The Treaty of Paris (1783) ending the Revolutionary War contained several provisions guaranteeing the rights of Loyalists and British creditors. These guarantees were made more explicit and were enlarged by Articles VI, IX, and X of the Jay Treaty. 8 Stat. 119-122.

106. See Richard E. Welch, *Theodore Sedgwick, Federalist* (Middletown: Wesleyan University Press, 1965), p. 107.

107. See, for example, *The Federalist,* No. 16.

108. In May 1791, a federal circuit court in Connecticut invalidated, as contrary to the Treaty of Peace of 1783, a statute of that state, which adversely affected the rights of British creditors to draw interest accruing during the Revolutionary War. This unreported case is mentioned by Warren, *Supreme Court in United States History,* I, 65-66. Other early cases involving claims of British creditors and denying the validity of sequestration statutes were *Brailsford* v. *Spalding* (United States Circuit Court in Georgia, 1792), and *Higginson* v. *Greenwood* (United States Circuit Court in South Carolina, 1793). In 1792 a Rhode Island statute providing for a three-year stay in actions for debt was declared unconstitutional by a federal circuit court in *Champion* v. *Casey.* None of these cases were reported, but there are bibliographic references in Warren, *Supreme Court in United States History,* I, 66-67.

109. *Georgia* v. *Brailsford,* 3 Dall. 1 (1794).

110. *Ware* v. *Hylton,* 3 Dall. 199 (1796).

111. *Fletcher* v. *Peck,* 6 Cranch 87 (1810).

112. *Fairfax's Devisee* v. *Martin's Lessee,* 7 Cranch 603 (1813).

Chapter 4

1. *Hollingsworth* v. *Virginia,* 3 Dall. 378 (1798).

2. Ibid., 379.

3. Ibid.

4. Ibid., 381.

5. *Cutting* v. *South Carolina* was continued.

6. *United States* v. *Peters,* 5 Cranch 115 (1809).

7. Ibid., 132. The text of the resolution passed by the Pennsylvania legislature on April 2, 1803, is set out in 5 Cranch 115, 123-134.

8. Ibid., 136.

9. Ibid., 139-140. As early as 1799 in *Fowler* v. *Lindsey*, 3 Dall. 411, the Court held that a state must be either nominally or substantially a party in order for the case to fall within the original jurisdiction of the Court. A state's incidental interest in the outcome does not suffice to oust the circuit court of jurisdiction in a controversy between private litigants over disputed land. The case involved, however, no plea under the Eleventh Amendment.

10. Of the seventeen states then in the Union, eleven responded with resolutions critical of Pennsylvania's action. Some explicitly asserted that the Supreme Court was the ultimate arbiter of constitutional questions, thereby replying to Pennsylvania's suggestion that a court should be created to settle disputes between the nation and the states. It has been suggested that the negative response of many states was occasioned by the secessionist movement in New England. See Charles G. Haines, *The Role of the Supreme Court in American Government and Politics, 1789-1835* (Berkeley: University of California Press, 1944), p. 138, and Charles Warren, *The Supreme Court in United States History* (Boston: Little, Brown, and Co., 1937), I, 373-383.

11. *United States* v. *Bright*, 24 Fed. Cas. 1237 (1809). In his opinion for the circuit court, Washington rejected the argument that the Eleventh Amendment was a defense on the ground that the amendment did not apply to cases in admiralty.

12. *Martin* v. *Hunter's Lessee*, 1 Wheat. 304 (1816).

13. *Cohens* v. *Virginia*, 6 Wheat. 264 (1821).

14. The defendants were at least presumed to be citizens of Virginia, for there was no averment to the contrary in the pleadings.

15. *Journal of the House of Delegates, Virginia* (1820), p. 108.

16. The resolution is quoted in Herman V. Ames, ed., *State Documents on Federal Relations* (Philadelphia: University of Pennsylvania, 1906), p. 104.

17. *Cohens* v. *Virginia*, 6 Wheat. 264, 290.

18. Ibid., 302-303.

19. Ibid., 306-307.

20. Ibid., 315.

21. Ibid., 347.

22. Ibid., 348-349.

23. Ibid., 351.

24. Ibid., 366-372.

25. Warren, *Supreme Court in United States History*, I, 550.

26. *Cohens* v. *Virginia*, 6 Wheat. 264, 380.

27. Ibid., 383.

28. "Were a state to lay a duty on exports, to collect the money and place it in her treasury, could a citizen who paid it, he asks, maintain a suit in this

court against such state to recover back the money? Perhaps not. Without, however, deciding such supposed case, we may say, that it is entirely unlike that under consideration." Ibid., 402.

29. Ibid., 403.

30. Ibid., 406-407.

31. Ibid., 407.

32. Ibid., 412.

33. *Hans* v. *Louisiana,* 134 U.S. 1 (1890).

34. After the Court's opinion sustaining its jurisdiction over the case, there was argument on the merits. Virginia declined to appear, but the Court heard Daniel Webster in support of the state judgment. Webster, it was explained, had been retained as counsel for the state of New York in a similar case. In a unanimous opinion by Chief Justice Marshall, the Court held that Congress had not authorized the city of Washington to sell lottery tickets in states prohibiting such sales. *Cohens* v. *Virginia,* 6 Wheat. 440.

35. *Niles Register* 21, p. 404.

36. Of special interest is John Taylor's *New Views on the Constitution of the United States* (Washington: Way and Gideon, 1823), in which he systematically attacked the Supreme Court for exercising political powers.

37. See Haines, *The Role of the Supreme Court,* pp. 440-441.

38. See Jefferson to Judge William Johnson, June 12, 1823, in *The Writings of Thomas Jefferson,* ed. Albert E. Bergh (Washington: Thomas Jefferson Association, 1905), XXV, 444-451.

39. Madison to Roane, May 6, 1821, in James Madison, *Letters and Other Writings of James Madison,* ed. Philip R. Fendall (Philadelphia: J. B. Lippincott and Co., 1867), III, 221-222.

40. *Smith* v. *Maryland,* 6 Cranch 286 (1810); *New Jersey* v. *Wilson,* 7 Cranch 164 (1812); and *McCulloch* v. *Maryland,* 4 Wheat. 316 (1819).

41. *Hans* v. *Louisiana,* 134 U.S. 1 (1890).

42. The Judiciary Act of 1875 was the first statute containing a provision that might be construed as generally permitting a suit against a state by one of its citizens. This provision gave the circuit courts "original cognizance, concurrent with the courts of the several states, of all suits of a civil nature at common law or in equity . . . arising under the Constitution, or laws of the United States, or treaties." Judiciary Act of 1875, 18 Stat. 470 (1875). Under this section *Hans* v. *Louisiana* was instituted.

43. Section 25 of the act, for all its generality, can hardly be construed to make a state amenable to original suit by its citizens where a federal claim is asserted. There seems to be no reported case in which a state was sued by one of its own citizens under the Judiciary Act of 1789, although there is a cloudy reference, in the records of the Pennsylvania legislature, to a suit by

one Thomas Proctor, a citizen of Pennsylvania, filed against the state in the circuit court. *Journal of the Pennsylvania House of Representatives* (1794-1795), p. 423. No record of the case has been found.

44. See Charles Warren, "New Light on the Federal Judiciary Act of 1789," *Harvard Law Review* 37 (November 1923): 93.

45. Ibid.

46. An Act to Establish the Judicial Courts of the United States, Section 13, c. 20, 1 Stat. 73, 80 (1789). (Italics mine.)

47. It is possible—but as previously suggested, unlikely (see pp. 42-43, above)—that Section 13 reflects a general supposition by Congress that the states were constitutionally immune from suit by any individual, citizen or not. If so, the phrase "except between a state and its citizens" may simply have been inserted to preclude a state, as plaintiff, from instituting in the Supreme Court a suit against one of its citizens where the suit arose under the Constitution. The possibility of such suits seems too fanciful to warrant this construction.

48. *Marbury* v. *Madison,* 1 Cranch 137 (1803), held that the original jurisdiction of the Court, as prescribed by the Constitution, could not be augmented by statute. That it could not be diminished by Congress was widely accepted as a corollary, although as early as 1793 Justice Wilson in circuit had held that the original jurisdiction of the Supreme Court was not exclusive. Congress might vest in other courts original jurisdiction over cases to which the Supreme Court's original jurisdiction was extended by the Constitution. Justice Iredell, dissenting, thought that the original jurisdiction of the Court was exclusive. *United States* v. *Ravara,* 2 Dall. 297 (1793). Chief Justice Marshall may have shared Iredell's view. See *Osborn* v. *Bank of United States,* 9 Wheat. 738, 821 (1824), but Wilson's interpretation was eventually approved by the Supreme Court in *Ames* v. *Kansas,* 111 U.S. 449, 469 (1884).

49. See, however, the dissent of Justice Johnson in *Governor of Georgia* v. *Madrazo,* 1 Pet. 110 (1828). Johnson read the exception "between a state and its citizens" as depriving the Supreme Court of original jurisdiction in cases falling within the judicial power of the United States and involving a state and one of its citizens as adverse parties. Thus, in admiralty and federal-question cases in which a state and a citizen thereof were arrayed in opposition, the Supreme Court would not have original jurisdiction. Such jurisdiction, he thought, was vested in inferior federal courts. Johnson, however, did not indicate that a state was suable in admiralty and federal-question cases. He was careful to emphasize that the state was the actor in this case.

50. It is remarkable—once the doctrine was established that the original

jurisdiction of the Supreme Court is not subject to congressional alteration—
that no suit by a citizen against his state was instituted in the Supreme Court.
If the federal-question clause were regarded as making a state amenable to
suit by its citizens, and if the original jurisdiction of the Court, by force of
constitutional provision alone, encompassed controversies "in which a state
shall be a party," it follows that such suits might be initiated in the Supreme
Court, notwithstanding the phrase "except between a state and its citizens"
in the Judiciary Act. The most obvious explanation for the failure of any
citizen to bring suit against a state in the Court is that the states were not
regarded as amenable to suit by individuals under the federal-question clause.

51. *Osborn* v. *Bank of the United States,* 9 Wheat. 738 (1824).

52. *McCulloch* v. *Maryland,* 4 Wheat. 316 (1819).

53. For an objective account of the background and facts of the *Osborn*
case, see Ernest L. Bogart, "Taxation of the Second Bank of the United
States by Ohio," *American Historical Review* 17 (1911-1912), 312-331.

54. Assertion of jurisdiction by the circuit court was the subject of an
elaborate report by a joint committee of the Ohio legislature issued late in
1820. The committee sharply challenged the power of the Supreme Court to
hear appeals from the state courts, and it undertook to refute Marshall's
reasoning in *McCulloch* v. *Maryland.* The committee report is more persuasive, however, in its argument that *Osborn* was, in fact, a proceeding against
the state of Ohio, which was precluded by the Eleventh Amendment. See
Annals of Congress, (16th Cong., 2d sess.), XXXVII, 1685-1714, for the text
of the report.

55. Reargument of *Osborn* was consolidated with argument in *Bank of the
United States* v. *Planters' Bank of Georgia,* 9 Wheat. 904 (1824). The
principal issue was whether the Bank of the United States had been authorized by its charter to sue in the circuit courts.

56. *Osborn* v. *Bank of the United States,* 9 Wheat. 738, 755.

57. Ibid., 803-804.

58. Ibid., 798.

59. Ibid. (Italics mine.)

60. Ibid., 799.

61. Ibid., 838.

62. It is clear that Marshall understood the bank to be a federal instrumentality. The processes of the federal government were, in his view, directly
threatened by Ohio's acts, and this provided a very strong reason for affording the bank with a federal judicial remedy. Whether Marshall intended to
extend to any individual a right to sue a state officer acting under an
unconstitutional statute is somewhat uncertain. Compare his language at pp.
847-848 with that at p. 857.

63. Ibid., 857.

64. Ibid., 738, 858. (Italics mine.)

65. The Court reversed the circuit court decree insofar as it awarded interest to the bank on a part of the money that had been seized. Ibid., 871.

66. *Governor of Georgia* v. *Madrazo,* 1 Pet. 110 (1828).

67. See Frankfurter, dissenting in *Larson* v. *Domestic & Foreign Corporation,* 337 U.S. 682, 711 (1949); Bernard Schwartz, *A Commentary on the Constitution of the United States* (New York: Macmillan Co., 1963) I, 400.

68. *Governor of Georgia* v. *Madrazo,* 1 Pet. 110, 123-124. (Italics mine.)

Chapter 5

1. The Act of April 20, 1871 (17 Stat. 13), gave the federal circuit and district courts original jurisdiction over "all suits authorized by law to redress the deprivation, under color of any law, statute, ordinance, regulation, custom or usage of any state, of any right, privilege, or immunity secured by the Constitution of the United States" without reference to the sum or value in controversy. This jurisdiction, however, was strictly construed by the Court in *Carter* v. *Greenhow,* 114 U.S. 317 (1885).

Of more immediate importance was the Act of March 3, 1875 (18 Stat. 470), extending the jurisdiction of the circuit courts to suits at common law or in equity "arising under the Constitution or laws of the United States" in which the amount in dispute was more than $500. This legislation was construed in *Hans* v. *Louisiana,* 134 U.S. 1 (1890).

For a concise summary of postwar legislation extending the jurisdiction of the federal courts, see Felix Frankfurter and James Landis, *The Business of the Supreme Court* (New York: Macmillan Co., 1928), pp. 61-69.

2. *Davis* v. *Gray,* 16 Wall. 203 (1873).

3. *Ex parte Young,* 209 U.S. 123 (1908).

4. *Cohens* v. *Virginia,* 6 Wheat. 264, 380 (1821); *Briscoe* v. *Bank of Kentucky,* 11 Pet. 257, 321 (1837).

5. As stated by the Court in *Minnesota* v. *Hitchcock,* 185 U.S. 373, 383 (1902), "the silence of counsel does not waive the question, nor would the express consent of the parties give to this court a jurisdiction which was not warranted by the Constitution and laws."

6. See Karl Singewald, *The Doctrine of Non-Suability of the State,* Johns Hopkins University Studies in Historical and Political Science, XXVIII (Baltimore: Johns Hopkins Press, 1910), p. 30.

7. *Smith* v. *Reeves,* 178 U.S. 436 (1900). In light of the disfavor into which the sovereign's exemption from suit has been said to have fallen, recent opinions of the Court strictly confining state waiver statutes to consent to

suit in state tribunals are somewhat surprising. See *Great Northern Insurance Co.* v. *Read,* 322 U.S. 47 (1944); *Ford Motor Co.* v. *Indiana Department of the Treasury,* 323 U.S. 459 (1945); and *Kennecott Copper Corp.* v. *Utah Tax Commission,* 327 U.S. 573 (1946). For a survey of waiver problems, see Richard Scatterday, "States-Waiver of Immunity to Suit," *Michigan Law Review* 45 (1947): 348.

8. *Hall* v. *Wisconsin,* 103 U.S. 5 (1880); *Clark* v. *Barnard,* 108 U.S. 436 (1883); *Gunter* v. *Atlantic Coast Line Railroad,* 200 U.S. 273 (1906).

9. See *Beers* v. *Arkansas,* 20 How. 527 (1858) and the concurring opinion by Justice Matthews for four members of the Court in *Antoni* v. *Greenhow,* 107 U.S. 769 (1883).

10. *Lincoln County* v. *Luning,* 133 U.S. 529 (1890).

11. Ibid., 530. Although the Eleventh Amendment does not bar suits against local governmental units in federal court, the liability of these units for acts of their officers is, of course, limited by other applicable principles. See *Hopkins* v. *Clemson College,* 221 U.S. 636, 646 (1911). Moreover, the fact that a county or city may be sued in federal court does not necessarily mean that local officers are subject to suit. If such an officer performs state functions, his immunity in a suit brought against him with reference to those functions is decided on the principles governing suits against state officers. *Ex parte Tyler,* 149 U.S. 164 (1893); *Graham* v. *Folsom,* 200 U.S. 248 (1906).

12. *Hans* v. *Louisiana,* 134 U.S. 1 (1890). To the same effect was *North Carolina* v. *Temple,* 134 U.S. 22, decided the same day, in which the Court reversed a decree of a federal circuit court directing the state and its auditor to pay a debt owed to the plaintiff.

13. Federal questions were incidentally decided by the circuit courts in the exercise of their diversity jurisdiction and in a few other situations, such as that involved in *Osborn* v. *Bank of United States,* where jurisdiction was specially conferred.

14. Act of March 3, 1875, 18 Stat. 470.

15. On this point Justice Harlan, concurring, took issue. *Chisholm,* he thought, had been correctly decided. *Hans* v. *Louisiana,* 134 U.S. 1, 21.

16. See above, pp. 96-97. For a different view, see Raoul Berger, *Congress v. The Supreme Court* (Cambridge: Harvard University Press, 1969), pp. 297-334.

17. See, however, Justice Frankfurter's dissent in *Larson* v. *Domestic & Foreign Corporation,* 337 U.S. 682, 710-723 (1949).

18. *Davis* v. *Gray,* 16 Wall. 203 (1873).

19. The grants to the company were conditioned upon survey, grading, and completion of construction of twenty-five miles of railroad lines. Construction was not completed within the time fixed by the original legislation

nor within the extended time limit allowed by later enactments. However, the Court attributed fault for the company's failure to perform to the state of Texas which, "by plunging into the war, and prosecuting it, confessedly rendered it impossible for the company to fulfill during its continuance." Ibid., 230.

20. Justice Davis, joined by Chief Justice Chase, dissented in a brief memorandum stating that the suit was, in effect, against the state of Texas. Justice Hunt did not participate.

21. *Davis* v. *Gray*, 16 Wall. 203, 220.

22. Very similar to the proceedings in *Davis* v. *Gray* were those in *Pennoyer* v. *McConnaughy*, 140 U.S. 1 (1891). Neither of these cases can be persuasively reconciled with the decisions in *Minnesota* v. *Hitchcock*, 185 U.S. 373 (1902), and *Oregon* v. *Hitchcock*, 202 U.S. 60 (1906), where the Court decided that suits brought against a federal officer to enjoin transfers of lands claimed by these states were suits against the United States.

23. *Board of Liquidation* v. *McComb*, 92 U.S. 531 (1876).

24. In Congress there was at least one attempt to repeal the Eleventh Amendment and to provide creditors with federal remedies against defaulting states. A constitutional amendment rescinding the Eleventh Amendment and empowering Congress "to provide by appropriate legislation for the legal enforcement of the obligation of contracts entered into by any of the states" was proposed in 1883. The resolution was not, however, reported by the House Judiciary Committee. *Congressional Record*, 47th Cong., 2d sess. (January 19, 1883), p. 1356.

25. A good early study of state repudiation is William A. Scott, *The Repudiation of State Debts* (New York: Thomas Y. Crowell and Co., 1893).

26. *Board of Liquidation* v. *McComb*, 92 U.S. 531, 541.

27. That part of the circuit court's order enjoining the issuance of any other bonds to the levee company was reversed. Ibid., 537.

28. *United States* v. *Lee*, 106 U.S. 196 (1882).

29. Specifically, the plaintiff claimed that tax commissioners had unlawfully made a general rule requiring, for redemption of property, the payment of delinquent taxes in person. According to the Court, the plaintiff was relieved of the necessity of making tender because of this general rule which deprived him of the right to redeem through an agent. Subsequent sale of the property by the commissioners to the United States could not, under these circumstances, extinguish his title.

30. *United States* v. *Lee*, 106 U.S. 196.

31. Ibid., 205-206.

32. Ibid., 207-208. (Italics mine.) The headnotes of *United States* v. *Lee*, which were written by Justice Miller, afford additional evidence that the

Court still adhered to the nominal-party rule: "(1) The doctrine that the United States cannot be sued by a party defendant in any court whatever, except where Congress has provided for such suit, examined and reaffirmed, and the nature of this exemption considered. (2) This exemption is, however, limited to suits against the United States directly and by name, and cannot be successfully pleaded in favor of officers and agents of the United States, when sued by private persons for property in their possession as such officers and agents."

33. Ibid., 220-221.

34. *Tindal* v. *Wesley*, 167 U.S. 204 (1897), applying the *Lee* principle in a suit against a state officer. However, where the proceeding against the officer tries the title claimed by the sovereign, immunity may be successfully pleaded. *Stanley* v. *Schwalby*, 147 U.S. 508 (1893); *Chandler* v. *Dix*, 194 U.S. 590 (1904). See also *Belknap* v. *Schild*, 161 U.S. 10 (1896), where the Court denied equitable relief against officers of the United States Navy in an action for infringement of plaintiff's patent on a caisson gate owned and used by the United States.

The compass of *United States* v. *Lee* has been severely restricted in recent opinions of the Court. *Larson* v. *Domestic & Foreign Corporation*, 337 U.S. 682 (1949), limited the *Lee* doctrine to situations where the plaintiff claimed that the defendant officer's occupancy constituted a taking of property without just compensation. And in *Malone* v. *Bowdoin*, 369 U.S. 643 (1962), the Court sustained the dismissal of an ejectment action against a forest service officer occupying land claimed by the plaintiff. Emphasis was placed upon the failure of the plaintiff to assert that occupancy constituted a taking, that the officer had exceeded his delegated powers, or that he was acting in anything other than his official capacity.

35. *New Hampshire* v. *Louisiana; New York* v. *Louisiana*, 108 U.S. 76 (1883).

36. Ibid., 89.

37. During oral argument, New York claimed that it was her right and duty as a state to protect her citizens against spoliation by another state. Since the Constitution had withdrawn from the states the sovereign powers of making war, imposing embargoes, and the like, the right to obtain a judicial settlement, which the Constitution had preserved, should be fully recognized. To this argument, the Court replied that the original Constitution, by affording, as against each state, a direct judicial remedy to citizens of other states, denied the indirect remedy whereby a state in order to defend the rights of its citizens, might sue another state. Although the Eleventh Amendment subsequently withdrew the direct remedy provided by the Constitution, the

indirect remedy was not revived. The Court's answer suggests that *Chisholm v. Georgia* was correctly decided—a view which it has rejected in other cases. See *Hans v. Louisiana.*

38. When, however, a citizen assigns to his state not only the bare legal title to a debt owed him by another state, but also his beneficial interest as well, a suit by that state against the debtor state is maintainable, as the Court ruled in *South Dakota v. North Carolina,* 192 U.S. 286 (1904). Four justices, however, dissented. A brief summary of some other attempts on the part of states receiving such assignments to enforce payment is in B. U. Ratchford, *American State Debts* (Durham: Duke University Press, 1941), pp. 239-240. In *Monaco v. Mississippi,* 292 U.S. 313 (1934), the Court denied a motion by a foreign state for leave to file suit against a state whose bonds had been assigned to it as an absolute gift.

39. *Louisiana ex. rel. Elliott v. Jumel,* 107 U.S. 711 (1883).

40. Ibid., 721.

41. Ibid., 727-728.

42. *Poindexter v. Greenhow,* 114 U.S. 270, 287 (1885); *Ex parte Ayers,* 123 U.S. 443, 487 (1887).

43. *Cunningham v. Macon Railroad,* 109 U.S. 446 (1883).

44. Ibid., 458-468. The dissenting justices argued that *United States v. Lee* required reversal of the lower court's decree.

45. Ibid., 451.

46. Ibid., 451-452.

47. Ibid., 453. With reference to *Davis v. Gray,* Justice Miller stated: "But it is clear that in enjoining the Governor of the State in the performance of one of his executive functions, the case goes to the verge of sound doctrine, if not beyond it, and that the principle should be extended no further. . . ."

48. Ibid., 457.

49. The dissenting opinion of Justice Bradley, with whom Chief Justice Waite, Justice Miller, and Justice Gray joined, in the *Virginia Coupon Cases,* 114 U.S. 270, 330 (1885), is the most cogent expression of this view.

50. Ibid., 331-332 (dissenting opinion).

51. There were seven cases in this series. In three of them, the plaintiffs were suing to recover property or damages, after officers of the state had seized their property in satisfaction of allegedly delinquent taxes. The plaintiffs had tendered coupons in payment of these taxes, but tender had been refused. *Poindexter v. Greenhow,* 114 U.S. 270 (1885); *Chaffin v. Taylor,* 114 U.S. 309 (1885); and *White v. Greenhow,* 114 U.S. 307 (1885). *Poindexter* and *Chaffin* reached the Court on writs of error from state courts,

while *White* came up from a federal circuit court. *Allen* v. *Baltimore and Ohio Railroad,* 114 U.S. 311 (1885), was a suit in equity to prevent collection of taxes by distraint upon the rolling stock and other property of the plaintiff company. In *Carter* v. *Greenhow,* 114 U.S. 317 (1885), and in *Pleasants* v. *Greenhow,* 114 U.S. 323 (1885), suits in law and in equity, respectively, brought under the Act of April 20, 1871, conferring jurisdiction in certain cases without regard to the amount in controversy, the Court dismissed the actions. See *n.* 1 above. Finally, there was *Marye* v. *Parsons,* 114 U.S. 325 (1885), in which the Court held that a coupon holder who did not allege that he was a taxpayer could not maintain a bill in equity to restrain tax collectors from refusing to accept such coupons.

52. The Virginia Funding Act of 1871 divided the public debt, amounting to $33 million, into two parts. One-third of the debt was attributed to West Virginia as its share of the overall indebtedness incurred before the two states were separated. Virginia acknowledged its obligation for the remaining two-thirds of the debt and issued new bonds, payable in thirty-four years, with interest at 6 percent, to fund its portion. Certificates were issued by Virginia in redemption of that portion of the bonded debt attributable to West Virginia, with Virginia agreeing to hold the surrendered bonds in trust for creditors and to pay them principal and interest "in accordance with such settlement as shall hereafter be made" between the two states. A settlement was not reached between the two states, but after protracted litigation beginning with *Virginia* v. *West Virginia,* 206 U.S. 290 (1907) and ending, on a somewhat inconclusive note, in *Virginia* v. *West Virginia,* 246 U.S. 565 (1918), the matter was resolved. In the latter case the Court determined that an earlier judgment, *Virginia* v. *West Virginia,* 238 U.S. 202 (1915), fixing West Virginia's liability, was enforceable, but the case was restored for argument on the question of implementing the judgment. In 1919, the West Virginia legislature enacted a statute providing for payment, in cash and bonds, to the state of Virginia, and with this the controversy ended.

53. *Hagood* v. *Southern,* 117 U.S. 52 (1886).

54. Cf. *Pennoyer* v. *McConnaughy,* 140 U.S. 1 (1891), at pp. 16-17, where the distinction between affirmative and negative relief is transmuted into full-blown constitutional doctrine.

55. *Hagood* v. *Southern,* 117 U.S. 52, 69.

56. *Ex parte Ayers,* 123 U.S. 443 (1887).

57. *Marye* v. *Parsons,* 114 U.S. 325 (1885).

58. *Ex parte Ayers,* 123 U.S. 443, 496.

59. Ibid., 489.

60. Justice Field, who had consistently voted with Harlan in previous cases, concurred separately in the decision of the Court. Harlan's dissenting

opinion, which was later to haunt him in *Ex parte Young*, emphasized that an action against an officer to enjoin him from bringing suit to enforce an unconstitutional statute is no more objectionable, on *jurisdictional* grounds, than an action enjoining him from seizing property. He admitted, however, that the latter case might justify an exercise of jurisdiction while the other might not. Ibid., 510-516.

61. Ibid., 500.

62. Most of the statutory provisions challenged in *Ex parte Ayers* were subsequently held to be unconstitutional in *McGahey* v. *Virginia*, 135 U.S. 662 (1890).

63. *Pennoyer* v. *McConnaughy*, 140 U.S. 1 (1891).

64. Ibid., 10.

65. Ibid., 16.

66. Moreover, with respect to claims asserted under the contract clause *Ex parte Ayers* was subsequently delimited in *Georgia Railroad & Banking Co.* v. *Redwine*, 342 U. S. 299 (1952), where the Court reversed the dismissal, by a three-judge federal court, of a proceeding to enjoin the state revenue commissioner from assessing or collecting certain taxes from which the corporation had been exempted by its charter. *Ayers* was construed as an action to compel specific performance of a state's contract while the proceeding in *Redwine* was portrayed as one to enjoin an unconstitutional invasion of property rights. The distinction is not sound; both cases can be viewed either way.

67. *Reagan* v. *Farmers Loan and Trust*, 154 U.S. 362 (1894).

68. *Ex parte Young*, 209 U.S. 123 (1908).

69. Law enforcement officers were enjoined by inferior federal courts from instituting criminal prosecutions in numerous cases filed after 1890. Prior to that year, such proceedings were rare. For citations to cases in which state officers were restrained from enforcing rate and liquor statutes, see Charles Warren, "Federal and State Court Interference," *Harvard Law Review* 43 (1930), 373n137.

70. *Prout* v. *Starr*, 188 U.S. 537 (1903).

71. One ground advanced in support of the jurisdiction of the circuit court was that the state had consented to suit. The statute creating the commission expressly authorized any dissatisfied railroad company or other interested party to file actions against the commission "in a court of competent jurisdiction in Travis County, Texas." The Court read this language as authorizing suit in the federal circuit court. But the principal independent ground for the decision was that even in the absence of such authorization the suit was not against the state. *Reagan* v. *Farmers Loan and Trust*, 154 U.S. 362, 392.

72. See, however, *n.*91 below.

73. *Reagan* v. *Farmers Loan and Trust,* 154 U.S. 362, 390.

74. *Smyth* v. *Ames,* 169 U.S. 466 (1898).

75. Ibid., 518-519.

76. *Fitts* v. *McGhee,* 172 U.S. 516 (1899).

77. *Prout* v. *Starr,* 188 U.S. 537 (1903).

78. Ibid., 544-545, citing *Harkrader* v. *Wadley,* 172 U.S. 148 (1898).

79. Ibid., 543. (Italics mine.)

80. *Ex parte Young,* 209 U.S. 123 (1908). Decided on the same day were *Hunter* v. *Wood,* 209 U.S. 205 (1908), and *General Oil Co.* v. *Crain,* 209 U.S. 211 (1908), both involving assertions of immunity under the Eleventh Amendment.

81. The order did not apply to enforcement of certain commodity rates fixed by the railroad commission or to passenger rates prescribed in another statute, because the railroads were complying with these. The circuit court noted, however, that the constitutional adequacy of the freight rates to which its order applied might be affected by the reasonableness of the other rates, and it reserved to final hearing, determination of that question. Ibid., 133.

82. Justice Harlan, it will be recalled, had dissented in nearly every case up to and including *Ex parte Ayers* in which relief was denied in suits against state officers. In cases in which relief was granted—including *Reagan, Smyth,* and *Prout*—he voted with the majority. But in *Fitts* v. *McGhee,* he wrote the opinion of the Court denying the requested relief. For him, even more than for other members of the Court, previous pronouncements were a source of embarrassment, as he conceded. Throughout his dissenting opinion, Harlan repeatedly stressed that those who framed and adopted the Eleventh Amendment "would have been amazed by the suggestion that a state can be prevented, by an order of a subordinate federal court, from being represented by its attorney general in a suit brought by it in one of its own courts." Ibid., 204.

83. Ibid., 148.

84. Ibid., 149-150.

85. Ibid., 155-156.

86. Ibid., 157-161.

87. Ibid., 163-164.

88. Ibid., 167.

89. Under the *Ayers* doctrine, however, the problem is avoided inasmuch as the wrong for which the officer is suable is not the impairment of the state's contract. The officer is suable for torts, and the limitation imposed upon state action by the contract clause becomes apposite only when the

officer pleads justification for his act by way of a law impairing the obligation of contracts.

90. The problem whether action by a state officer or by a subdivision of a state is state action within the meaning of the Fourteenth Amendment received attention in *Barney* v. *New York*, 193 U.S. 430 (1904); *Siler* v. *Louisville Railroad*, 213 U.S. 175 (1909); and *Home Telephone Co.* v. *Los Angeles*, 227 U.S. 278 (1913). In the *Home Telephone* case, the Court recognized the problem which a strict state-action interpretation of the Fourteenth Amendment poses in suits against state officers. See also *Iowa-Des Moines Bank* v. *Bennett*, 284 U.S. 239 (1931).

91. That federal judicial protection was expedited by allowing direct access to the circuit courts is clear. But it was significantly expanded also. If those contesting the constitutionality of rates prescribed by the state had been required to raise the issue first in the state courts, federal judicial protection would have been available only by way of a writ of error from the Supreme Court of the United States. The constitutional sufficiency of rates, however, is largely a fact question, which a writ of error, instead of present-ing, theoretically forecloses. See Charles Warren, "Federal and State Court Interference," *Harvard Law Review* 43 (1930), 375-376.

92. *Ogden* v. *Saunders*, 12 Wheat. 213 (1827).

93. Benjamin F. Wright, Jr., *The Contract Clause of the Constitution* (Cambridge: Harvard University Press, 1938), p. 91 ff.

94. For various aspects of this development, see Edward S. Corwin, *Liberty Against Government* (Baton Rouge: Louisiana State University Press, 1948); Clyde E. Jacobs, *Law Writers and the Courts* (Berkeley: University of California Press, 1954); Robert G. McCloskey, *American Conservatism in the Age of Enterprise* (Cambridge: Harvard University Press, 1951); Arnold Paul, *Conservative Crisis and the Rule of Law* (Ithaca: Cornell University Press, 1960); Sidney Fine, *Laissez Faire and the General-Welfare State* (Ann Arbor: University of Michigan Press, 1956).

95. *Congressional Record*, 60th Cong., 1st sess. (April 17, 1908), p. 4847. The reference was to events in North Carolina where resentment against the federal judiciary was intense at the time. This feeling appears to have been due not so much to *Ex parte Young* as to the decision in *McNeill* v. *Southern Railroad*, 202 U.S. 543 (1906), in which the Court upheld a decree of the United States Circuit Court for the Eastern District of North Carolina prohibiting the enforcement of certain orders of the state corporation com-mission. These orders were challenged as violative of the commerce clause. In *Hunter* v. *Wood*, 209 U.S. 205 (1908), decided on the same day as *Ex parte Young*, the Court disposed of another aspect of the litigation considered in *McNeil*.

96. *Ex parte Young,* 209 U.S. 123, at 163. The Court did not specifically mention the Act of March 2, 1793 (1 Stat. 335), which forbade any court of the United States from granting "a writ of injunction to stay proceedings in any court of a state." To this prohibition, later statutes introduced a few exceptions, such as that allowing the issuance of federal injunctions in bankruptcy proceedings (36 Stat. 1162). Although the 1793 act, if literally read, applies only to injunctions directed to a state court, judicial interpretation of this legislation broadened its coverage to include decrees enjoining state officers from pursuing actions pending in the state courts. *Harkrader* v. *Wadley,* 172 U.S. 148 (1898); *Gunter* v. *Atlantic Coast Line Railroad,* 200 U.S. 273 (1906). As Warren, "Federal and State Court Interference," pp. 374-375, indicates, the *Young* decision, in sanctioning federal injunctions restraining state officers from instituting suits in state courts, created the same frictions and hostility that the Act of 1793 was intended to prevent.

97. An interesting account of one such incident is by Senator Crawford of South Dakota in *Congressional Record,* 61st Cong., 2d sess., (June 2, 1910), p. 7252.

98. *Prentis* v. *Atlantic Coast Railroad,* 211 U.S. 210 (1908).

99. A version of the bill providing for stays of federal court proceedings where the state instituted a test case in its own courts was later incorporated into the Act of March 4, 1913 (37 Stat. 1013).

100. For a penetrating critique of federal equity practice following *Young,* see Joseph Hutcheson, "A Case for Three Judges," *Harvard Law Review* 47 (1934), 800-810.

101. *Congressional Record,* 61st Cong., 2d sess. (June 2, 1910), p. 7256.

102. Act of June 18, 1910, 36 Stat. 557. The rider was introduced on June 2 by Senator Overman of North Carolina. *Congressional Record,* 61st Cong., 2d sess., pp. 7253-7254. During debate, the Senator remarked that the bill had the support of the Judiciary Committee, the Attorney General of the United States, and the attorneys general of every state. A similar bill was approved by the Senate in 1908 but it was not finally enacted. *Congressional Record,* 60th Cong., 1st sess., (April 17, 1908), pp. 4846-4859.

103. The vote was 33 in favor to 28 opposed, with 31 senators not voting. *Congressional Record,* 61st Cong., 2d sess., (June 2, 1910), p. 7258.

104. *Philadelphia County* v. *Stimson,* 223 U.S. 605 (1912).

105. *Larson* v. *Domestic & Foreign Corporation,* 337 U.S. 682 (1949), in which the Court, on immunity grounds, declined to afford specific relief against a federal officer for acts which, though wrongful, were not *ultra vires* nor pursuant to an unconstitutional statute.

106. *Ex parte New York,* 256 U.S. 490 (1921).

107. *Sterling* v. *Constantin,* 287 U.S. 378 (1932).

Chapter 6

1. *Chisholm* v. *Georgia,* 2 Dall. 419, 435 (1793).

2. See Justice Miller's opinion for the Court in *United States* v. *Lee,* 106 U.S. 196, 208 (1882).

3. Robert D. Watkins, *The State as a Party Litigant,* Johns Hopkins University Studies in Historical and Political Science, XLV (Baltimore: Johns Hopkins Press, 1927), p. 193.

4. *Nicholl* v. *United States,* 7 Wall. 122, 126 (1869).

5. *Larson* v. *Domestic & Foreign Corporation,* 337 U.S. 682, 704 (1949).

6. *Ex parte Young,* 209 U.S. 123 (1908).

7. *Philadelphia County* v. *Stimson,* 223 U.S. 605 (1912).

8. *Larson* v. *Domestic & Foreign Corporation,* 337 U.S. 682 (1949).

9. *Pennoyer* v. *McConnaughy,* 140 U.S. 1 (1891).

10. *Georgia Railroad & Banking Company* v. *Redwine,* 342 U.S. 299, 304 (1952).

11. *Kawananakoa* v. *Polybank,* 205 U.S. 349, 353 (1907).

12. *Griffin* v. *School Board of Prince Edward County,* 377 U.S. 218 (1964). *Brief of Respondent: Griffin* v. *School Board,* pp. 7-18.

13. The county board of supervisors, the county treasurer, the state board of education, and the state superintendent of public instruction were also defendants in these proceedings.

14. *Griffin* v. *School Board of Prince Edward County,* 377 U.S. 218, 228.

15. *Hawaii* v. *Gordon,* 373 U.S. 57, 58 (1963).

16. *Dugan* v. *Rank,* 372 U.S. 609, 620 (1963), citing *Land* v. *Dollar,* 330 U.S. 731, 738 (1947), *Larson* v. *Domestic & Foreign Corporation,* 337 U.S. 682, 704 (1949), and *Ex parte New York,* 256 U.S. 490, 502 (1921).

17. See Kenneth C. Davis, *Administrative Law Treatise* (St. Paul: West Publishing Co., 1958), III (Supp., 1965, p. 149).

18. The Court, at the conclusion of its opinion, specifically held that the decree of the district court might direct that public schools be reopened and that the board of supervisors levy taxes "to raise funds adequate to reopen, operate, and maintain without racial discrimination a public school system in the county." *Griffin* v. *School Board of Prince Edward County,* 377 U.S. 218, 233. Justices Clark and Harlan dissented from the holding that the federal courts could order reopening of the schools.

19. *Ex parte New York,* 256 U.S. 490, 500 (1921).

20. *Pennoyer* v. *McConnaughy,* 140 U.S. 1 (1891).

21. *Board of Liquidation* v. *McComb,* 92 U.S. 531, 541 (1876); *Rolston* v. *Crittenden,* 120 U.S. 390, 411 (1887).

22. *Louisiana* v. *Jumel,* 107 U.S. 711 (1883).

23. *United States ex rel. Goldberg* v. *Daniels,* 231 U.S. 218 (1913); *Minnesota* v. *United States,* 305 U.S. 382 (1939).

24. *Great Northern Insurance Co.* v. *Read,* 322 U.S. 47, 50 (1944); *Mine Safety Appliance Co.* v. *Forrestal,* 326 U.S. 371 (1945); *Lankford* v. *Platte Iron Works Co.,* 235 U.S. 461 (1915).

25. *United States* v. *Lee,* 106 U.S. 196 (1882).

26. *Malone* v. *Bowdoin,* 369 U.S. 643 (1962).

27. *Larson* v. *Domestic & Foreign Corporation,* 337 U.S. 682, 709 (1949)

28. Ibid., 710-723. A critique of Justice Frankfurter's analysis is in Davis, *Administrative Law Treatise,* III, 571-576.

29. Milton M. Carrow in his perceptive article, "Sovereign Immunity in Administrative Law," *Journal of Public Law* 9 (1960), 1-23, identifies four factors, which appear to account for decisions regarding immunity: (1) the form of the judicial remedy; (2) the kind of administrative action challenged; (3) the type of interest affected; and (4) the character of the agency or official sued. But no principle or set of principles rationalizes the results actually reached in the various cases.

30. *Keifer & Keifer* v. *Reconstruction Finance Corporation,* 306 U.S. 381, 388 (1939).

31. See, for example, *Hans* v. *Louisiana,* 134 U.S. 1 (1890), and *Williams* v. *United States,* 289 U.S. 553 (1933).

32. Presumably Justice Iredell would have sustained the immunity of the United States if that question had been presented, but the attitudes of the other members of the Court at the time are far from clear. Both Chief Justice Jay and Justice Cushing stated—rather equivocally—that the United States might be exempt from suit, but each left the question open. *Chisholm* v. *Georgia,* 2 Dall. 419, 469, 478. Justices Wilson and Blair refrained from comment on the question, but their general approach suggests that in a proper case they might have denied to the United States the sovereign exemption.

33. In *Ex parte Young* the questions as to the propriety of federal judicial control over state officers in the enforcement of state policies were revived and received brief attention; such questions have also been considered as the Court has developed the abstention doctrine and other restraints upon the powers of inferior federal courts.

34. *Keifer & Keifer* v. *Reconstruction Finance Corporation,* 306 U.S. 381, 396 (1939).

35. This is not to imply the judicialization of relief for every wrong. There are various limits upon the judicial process, such as administrative finality, justiciability, and ripeness—restrictions upon the judicial determination of

issues which are much more intelligible and defensible than the immunity doctrine. Moreover, even if the immunity of the sovereign from suit were renounced, the government might continue to fix the limits of its liability, insofar as such enactments were not violative of constitutional guarantees.

36. *National City Bank* v. *Republic of China*, 348 U.S. 356, 360 (1955).

37. In *Molitor* v. *Kaneland Community Unit District*, 18 Ill. 2d 11, the Supreme Court of Illinois repudiated the immunity doctrine, although the state constitution expressly declares that "the state shall never be made defendant in any court of law or equity." Comment on recent state judicial trends with respect to sovereign immunity and tort liability is in Davis, *Administrative Law Treatise*, III (Supp., 1965, pp. 95-109).

Bibliographic Note

The notes to this study include bibliographic data on materials that were consulted, and this note will not attempt to cover all these sources. A few secondary works and most of the primary sources deserve, for their importance, some comment.

A solid and perceptive analysis of the origins and development of the immunity doctrine in English law is in Sir William Holdsworth, *A History of English Law* (London: Methuen, 1944). An excellent and highly influential, although specially focused, study of sovereign immunity in the United States, with extensive references to primary and secondary sources, is Edwin M. Borchard's "Government Liability in Tort," *Yale Law Journal* 34 (1924-1925), 1-43, 129-143, 229-258; 36 (1926-1927), 1-41, 757-807, 1039-1100. A more recent analysis and incisive critique of sovereign immunity is in Kenneth C. Davis, *Administrative Law Treatise* (St. Paul: West, 1958, 1965 supp.).

While secondary works on sovereign immunity are numerous, the Eleventh Amendment has not been the object of much systematic treatment. There is no book-length study of the amendment, although Karl Singewald's monograph, *The Doctrine of Non-Suability of the State in the United States*, Johns Hopkins

Studies in Historical and Political Science, XXVIII (Baltimore: Johns Hopkins Press, 1910), includes brief discussion of the origins of the amendment and an extended analysis of some judicial applications of that instrument. A few articles in professional journals deal with the origins of the amendment, most notably Allen C. Braxton's "The Eleventh Amendment," *Virginia State Bar Association Report* 20 (1907), 172-193, and William D. Guthrie's "The Eleventh Amendment," *Columbia Law Review* 8 (1908), 183-207. Neither of these works, however, are satisfactory historical studies. Important new light on the background of the Eleventh Amendment is provided by Doyle Mathis, "Chisholm v. Georgia: Background and Settlement," *Journal of American History* 54 (1967), 19-29, and the unreported and partially reported cases contemporaneous with *Chisholm* v. *Georgia* are considered in my "Prelude to Amendment: The States Before the Court," *American Journal of Legal History* 12 (1968), 19-40.

Primary sources used in preparing the last three chapters of this book are principally the reported judicial cases, and those cited in the text and footnotes are indexed in the Table of Cases. The first three chapters—discussing the genesis and development of Article III of the Constitution, the reception of this article during the period of ratification, the early judicial cases in which states were impleaded as defendants, and the proceedings attendant upon adoption of the Eleventh Amendment—are based upon a wider range of sources.

For materials on the framing of the Federal Constitution, Max Farrand, ed., *The Records of the Federal Convention,* first published in three volumes in 1911 and republished with a fourth volume in 1937 (Yale University Press), remains the standard reference. In addition to Madison's *Journal,* these volumes include a large number of documents illustrating the evolution of various constitutional provisions.

Jonathan Elliot's *Debates in the Several State Conventions on the Adoption of the Federal Constitution,* 2d ed. (Philadelphia:

Lippincott, 1876) remains useful, although the records are incomplete. The *Records of the States* (microfilm) of the Library of Congress contains additional material on state convention proceedings (see Library of Congress, *A Guide to the Microfilm Collection of Early State Records*). Moreover, the records of proceedings in the conventions of certain states have been compiled in such works as John B. McMaster and Frederick D. Stone, eds., *Pennsylvania and the Federal Constitution, 1787-1788* (Philadelphia: Historical Society of Pennsylvania, 1888), which also includes contemporaneous essays and other materials. Essays, pamphlets, and polemical comments on the proposed Constitution are included in Paul Ford, ed., *Essays on the Constitution* (Brooklyn: Historical Printing Club, 1892) and in his *Pamphlets on the Constitution, 1787-1788* (Brooklyn: 1888). Cecelia M. Kenyon, ed., *The Antifederalists* (Indianapolis: Bobbs-Merrill, 1966) is a more recent collection. The most important contemporaneous defense is, of course, *The Federalist* by Hamilton, Madison, and Jay, which is readily accessible in many editions.

The official reports by Alexander Dallas of the early cases in which the Supreme Court asserted jurisdiction over suits by individuals against various states are incomplete and inaccurate. Information concerning proceedings in these cases is in the *Minutes of the Supreme Court* and the *Dockets of the Supreme Court* for the period 1790-1798. The originals of these documents, available on microfilm, are in the National Archives, and the *Minutes* have been printed in the *American Journal of Legal History* 5-8 (1961-1964). The facts of these cases, which are unstated or obscure in both the official reports and the *Minutes,* may be gleaned from materials in the official case files, also in the National Archives. The usefulness of these materials is somewhat impaired by their condition. Many of the documents were damaged by fire and water during the late nineteenth century.

Two important pamphlets were an immediate consequence of the first case in which a state was sued in the Supreme Court.

James Sullivan, *Observations Upon the Government of the United States of America* (Boston: Samuel Hall, 1791) and Hortensius [Timothy Ford], *An Inquiry into the Constitutional Authority of the Supreme Court Over the Several States in Their Political Capacity* (Charleston: W. P. Young, 1792), the first challenging and the other defending the Court's assertion of jurisdiction, are among the most interesting constitutional pamphlets of the 1790s.

The proceedings of the state legislatures throw light on the official reaction of many of the states to the early cases, especially to *Chisholm* v. *Georgia*. Here again the Library of Congress' *Records of the States* (microfilm) for the period 1790-1798 is a major source. The records, while incomplete for certain states and not as detailed as the researcher might hope, are invaluable. The same source may be consulted for state action ratifying the Eleventh Amendment. For proceedings in Congress with reference to proposal of the amendment, the *Annals of Congress* disclose motions and votes but, unfortunately, the debates were unreported.

For additional light on the meaning of the disputed clause of Article III and on the purposes of those who participated in the adoption of the Eleventh Amendment, the published correspondence and writings of the statesmen, politicians, and judges of the period are an obvious, but generally disappointing source. There are only scattered references to these matters in such works, and those few having any importance to this study are cited in the notes.

Table of Cases

Index